ENEMY OF THE SUN

ENEMY OF THE SUN

Poetry of Palestinian Resistance

Edited by
NASEER ARURI and EDMUND GHAREEB

Preface by
GREG THOMAS

Seven Stories Press
New York • Oakland • London

Originally published by Drum & Spear Press.

Seven Stories Press
140 Watts Street
New York, NY 10013
www.sevenstories.com

Library of Congress Cataloging-in-Publication Data

Names: Aruri, Naseer Hasan, 1934-2015, editor. | Ghareeb, Edmund, editor. | Thomas, Greg, 1969- writer of preface.
Title: Enemy of the sun : poetry of Palestinian resistance / edited by Naseer Aruri and Edmund Ghareeb ; preface by Greg Thomas.
Description: 2025 edition. | New York : Seven Stories Press, 2025.
Identifiers: LCCN 2024053857 (print) | LCCN 2024053858 (ebook) | ISBN 9781644214558 (trade paperback) | ISBN 9781644214565 (ebook)
Subjects: LCSH: Arabic poetry--Palestine--Translations into English. | LCGFT: Poetry.
Classification: LCC PJ8190.65.E5 E54 2025 (print) | LCC PJ8190.65.E5 (ebook) | DDC 892.7/160889274--dc23/eng/20241214
LC record available at https://lccn.loc.gov/2024053857
LC ebook record available at https://lccn.loc.gov/2024053858

College professors and high school and middle school teachers may order free examination copies of Seven Stories Press titles. Visit https://www.sevenstories.com/pg/resources-academics or email academic@sevenstories.com.

Printed in the United States of America

9 8 7 6 5 4 3 2

CONTENTS

THE POETS AND THEIR POEMS

MAHMOUD DARWEESH

RASHED HUSSEIN

*Dedicated to the long suffering and steadfastness
of the Palestinian people.*

THE WEAPON OF POETRY

PREFACE TO THE 2025 EDITION

This book is a gem and a marvel. What fool would want to live without it? We are truly indebted to all these poets as well as editors Naseer Aruri and Edmund Ghareeb for their collective labor of love. Where else today can we enjoy such a stunning literary line-up in Arabic-to-English translation? The value of this volume has no doubt increased over time. Reading or re-reading these beautiful and powerful poems, one might find it astounding that such an important collection could remain out of print for over half a century! One can only assume that this disappearance was the result of an ongoing counter-revolution against the epic 1960s along with the general colonial-imperial fear of the militant Black and Palestinian solidarity which first brought about this publication via Drum & Spear Press in 1970—just in time to reach the prison cell of George Jackson, the immortal Field Marshal of the Black Panther Party.

I first stumbled upon this book while conducting research for a book project on Jackson's writings from prison and the discovery changed the course of everything. Only part of this story is now more or less familiar to some. One day in California, I came across a strange document while rummaging through old legal files in the office of a lawyer who had represented one of the defendants in the big "San Quentin Six" trial in the early-to-mid 1970s. It turned out to be a list of items seized from the prison cell of "Comrade George" after his assassination by agents of the state on August 21, 1971. The other prisoners who resisted state massacre with him—for "a half hour of freedom," as they say— had their cells searched by armed guards too. The lists compiled for them were short notations of pretty negligible content. By contrast, this document was several pages long and remarkably homogeneous, recording books upon books in the possession of an embattled Black revolutionary. No bourgeois library or practice of "book worship," in the well-known words of Mao Zedong, it was instead a partial bibliography of his praxis and revolutionary critical engagements. On first count, there were ninety-nine books literally covered in blood—the blood of racist state murder and anti-racist prisoner resistance. Two weeks later, the tally was adjusted to account for twenty-six in addition to a catalog. All in all, they formed a crucial part of Jackson's last year of work on *Blood in My Eye*, his second book manuscript which was smuggled out for publication, past both reactionary prison administrators and white liberal-editorial censorship, merely weeks before his martyrdom.

The 1971 catalog closing out this list was identified as "Catalog #3" of Drum & Spear Bookstore. Of course, the same Drum & Spear complex had produced the ninety-third item of this documentary memo to Warden "Red" Nelson: *Enemy of the Sun* by Naseer Aruri-Edmund Ghareeb. At that point, I only half-recognized the abbreviated title from my previous leafings through the Black Panther Party's newspaper. It rang a bell. I had to order one of the few copies of the book still available online to see its subtitle: "Poetry of Palestinian Resistance." Soon I returned to old issues of the paper. Once again, I saw that large double-page inset unfolding as a centerpiece spread, perhaps a detachable poster in memoriam, which featured a color photograph of the BPP Field Marshal next to two columns of poetic verse with the caption: "'Enemy of the Sun' by George Jackson." Somehow, Sameeh Al-Qassem's poem had become George Jackson's poem. Over the next few decades, this classic poem from Palestine would become known as a Black poem from Black America. To be sure, there is something totally mystical about this scenario. But we could begin to explain how what I've dubbed "a magical mistake of revolutionary solidarity and kinship" took place between Drum &

Spear Press, San Quentin Prison as a site of resistance, and *The Black Panther Intercommunal News Service.*

This was the story I told as curator of the exhibit "George Jackson in the Sun of Palestine," which opened on October 20, 2015, at the museum of the Abu Jihad Center for Prisoner Movement Affairs on the Abu Dis campus of Al Quds University. The caged Panther must have written down some of the poems from *Enemy of the Sun* to share with comrades in and/or outside of prison. And in the chaotic aftermath of his assassination, these transcriptions must have easily been mistaken for his own writings. The voices are strikingly similar indeed. While Mrs. Georgia Jackson immediately scrambled to retrieve her son's intellectual property from the prison establishment, his political party would continue to publish and reprint his writings in its newspaper after a noteworthy period of clandestine correspondence between him and its Minister of Defense, Huey P. Newton.

When I shared this information with Zakaria Zubeidi during an interview in the West Bank, he laughed as he recalled how he and fellow captives used to write down words from any part of the world (oftentimes unattributed to any particular source) on anything from prison walls to toilet paper. What's more, a childhood friend of Naji Al-Ali notes in Kasim Abid's documentary film *Naji Al-Ali: An Artist with Vision* that in prison, the iconic Palestinian cartoonist used to write or draw *on him*: "He was always drawing—on anything—even my trousers. He used to ask me to sit down and he would draw on them. He drew on anything he could, on hands, legs, everywhere." However George Jackson circulated "Enemy of the Sun," we can say without question that he was reiterating what Frantz Fanon once called the "brotherhood of the prison's quicklime."

The connection to this poetry book was quite expansive, going far beyond the one poem chosen by editors for the title of this collection. When Watan Al-Qassem attended our exhibition opening in Abu Dis, he pointed out that the main Black Panther newspaper image on display ("'Enemy of the Sun' by George

Jackson") actually reproduces verses from three of his father's poems: "I Defy" and "Farewell in Sophia" as well as "Enemy of the Sun." The two-column text was therefore a composite of the Sameeh Al-Qassem section of the *Enemy of the Sun* anthology. Interestingly enough, research shows that the poem "Enemy of the Sun" was itself known by another title: "Address from the Unemployment Bureau." At any rate, the content and refrain of this poem have proven as irresistible, historically, as the collection as a whole. Shortly before his murder by the state, leaving no authorial mystery whatsoever, George Jackson wrote in a *Black Panther* article critiquing prisoner defense committee liberalism: "I have been a condemned man all my life—just like you all. But I doomed myself to free and aggressive action and have made it quite plain to the 'Enemy of the Sun' that I will oppose him until he proves stronger, to the death of them or us."

How many art exhibitions have been based on a single book? In this case, the book is one that links two oppressed and exploited peoples whose resistance struggles are legendary in and beyond literature. Our graphic designer, Jonelle Davies, created a gorgeous series of six giant posters based on the original cover design of *Enemy of the Sun: Poetry of Palestinian Resistance*. They introduced the exhibition in both English and Arabic and stimulated further interest in the history of the long out-of-print book. For some time, it was very difficult to share these poems. I had to photocopy them and scan them at high resolution. Everyone was always asking about them, especially after hearing the story at the center of this traveling exhibition. To read, to teach, to study, to preserve, to mobilize.

The art exhibit, titled "George Jackson in the Sun of Palestine," moved across Palestine as well as Europe and North America and was mounted in Gaza on August 16–17, 2022, before the Israeli backlash against Operation Al-Aqsa Flood. I worked with independent scholar Muhammad Ismael of the General Union of Palestinian Writers and a few others to make it happen against all kinds of odds. As he'd report on this rather historic success: "Attendance wasn't only quantitatively but also qualitatively impressive.

Besides a few members of the YMCA Board of Directors, a lot of writers, poets, literary critics, painters, historians, academics, and teachers were present. Moreover, several retired Fedayeen visited as well—namely, Fedayeen of the *Fahd Aswad* (Black Panther cadres) in Gaza, Fedayeen of PFLP, and Fedayeen of the Palestinian Popular Struggle Front." It was as if the pages and readership of *Enemy of the Sun* had opened up to become a festival of life and struggle in a new day and another place. Indeed, Nizar Qabbani could have been writing to them from this priceless text itself:

> *Poets of the occupied land,*
> *You are the prettiest birds to fly out of captivity*
> *Pure, like the prayers of the dawn*
> *You are the roses growing from within the flame*
> *You are the rain falling despite repression and defeat*
> *You taught us how the drowned can sing*
> *from the bottom of the sea*
> *and how the grave can stand and walk*

One special presence in Gaza City was the great poet-warrior Saleem Al-Naffar, also of the General Union of Palestinian Writers, who recited his own "resistance poetry" throughout the exhibition program. Tragically, most of this local exhibition team would be martyred by the Zionist genocidal warfare against all Palestinians in the Strip: Saleem's son, Mustafa Al-Naffar (photographer); Ahmad Ismael (graphic artist); and Saleem Al-Naffar himself. Despite these massacres, the struggle steadfastly continues—for life and memory, liberation and self-determination, solidarity and more. The post-exhibition connections have continued to bear fruit in ways that cannot be minimized or underestimated, as evidenced by Mumia Abu-Jamal's own radio program and article on our persistent work titled "Black in Gaza."

Enemy of the Sun initially came to us in a "Poets of Liberation" series. As Audre Lorde reminds us, "Poetry is not a luxury." Let us recall that the original preface to this volume was written by Samuel W. Allen, a veteran Pan-Africanist scholar who himself wrote poetry under the pen name Paul Vesey. Through Richard Wright and his own work on Negritude, Allen had an affiliation with Présence Africaine, the eminent Black diasporic journal and bookstore which served as an inspiration for the creation of the Drum & Spear Bookstore in Washington, DC. Allen led a very insightful discussion of the "new" poetry of the Black Arts Movement and its iconoclastic identification with Palestine as we prepared to encounter the twelve poets of the original 1970 edition of this collection: Rashed Hussein, Tawfiq Zayyad, Salem Jubran, Nizar Qabbani, Fadwa Touqan, Arshad Tawfiq, Yusif Hamdan, Abdel Rahman Muhammad Rafie, Hadia Abdul-Hadi, and Fawzi Jiryis Abdullah, as well as Mahmoud Darweesh and Sameeh Al-Qassem. It is a wonder to look back on these creative artists, their careers, and their contributions to poetry and liberation now from the vantage point of the twenty-first century.

Recently, I found myself at a presentation on political poster art and Palestine solidarity in Belgium. There on stage in Brussels, Lucas Catherine recounted his experience of hanging out with Sameeh Al-Qassem when visiting the city of Haifa some years ago. He ended up spending the night at the poet's village home in Rama and waking up the next morning to Al-Qassem *blasting* Nina Simone's "Don't Let Me Be Misunderstood"! How appropriate, I thought, and absolutely thrilling to hear after learning how some of his "resistance poetry" came to live a long Black life in the context of North America thanks to the Black Radical Tradition of veteran SNCC organizers who founded Drum & Spear Press, as well as George L. Jackson and the Black Panther Party.

Jean Genet famously wrote in his introduction to *Soledad Brother: The Prison Letters of George Jackson* that it was not a book but "a weapon," a "striking poem of love and of combat." Genet's reflections on the fedayeen were frequently poetic as well. He would go on to maintain in articles collected posthumously in *The Declared Enemy: Texts and Interviews* that revolution was "impossible" without the poetry of revolt "that precedes it." In his revolutionary practice, Comrade George gave us what Amílcar Cabral called "the weapon of theory" as well as the *weapon of poetry*. This reappearance of *Enemy of the Sun* finally makes all its poetic resources available again for generations old and new. The book was already an icon even while out of print for decades. What an audience it has in store now. Ages ago, its poetic language entered the piercing vocabulary of a pantheon of revolutionaries such as Amiri Baraka, Dhoruba Bin Wahad, and Safiya Bukhari. On September 23, 2020, Elaine Brown and Michel Khleifi recited "Enemy of the Sun" online in English and Arabic for a Radio Alhara program airing from Bethlehem which I co-organized with Viktoria Metschl to encourage celebrations of George Jackson's birthday (beyond commemorations of his assassination) across the globe. These days, the poem can be heard at activist demonstrations anywhere. For Genet, like Lorde, poetry means something like metamorphosis, knowing and feeling, human spirit, transformation and transcendence. It is a prelude to the revolutionary liberation we need. And this classic collection of Palestinian resistance poetry demonstrates as much in abundance.

GREG THOMAS
Oakland, California
May 2024

PREFACE TO THE 1970 EDITION

Tragedy is accepted to mean a sequence of events seemingly inevitable, exciting pity and fear and leading to disaster. It is hard to escape the chilling impression that this describes the state of affairs in the Middle East. Not simply is our compassion invoked for the victims of that drama, and there are legitimate demands on either side for that—but there is a leitmotif of derailment—of unfixable outofjointedness; the times, and the place, are out of joint and no one has the tools to mend them. There is something epochal and larger than the lives of the immediate unhappy participants in this sanguinary clash of Arab and of Jew, a fateful overcast through which the rest of us peer apprehensively as the tragedy unfolds. It is with fascination but also a gloomy sense of irreducible conflict that we read these poems.

The problems of translation are, as always with poetry, considerable. English, which Stephen Spender points out is at its best only with a certain awkwardness, was not designed to describe the curved blade of the Saracen. Nonetheless, Naseer Aruri and Edmund Ghareeb have obviously labored with skill and thoroughly, and most of this poetry comes through with clarity and persuasion. It is wide in its range and varied in texture. Without yielding to the clichés of desert, mosque, and sultan, one hears, yet, echoes of the passion of the Fertile Crescent in this poetry. In this technical and reasoned society, disjointed though it may be in this civilization of the reactor and the gyroscope, the blood has been let out of office. It is old and tired, or it is suspect. It would be a withered soul, however, who did not respond to the passionate and moving witness of national purpose in much of this collection. It may be true that the poets—Al-Qassem, Qabbani, Darweesh, Hussein, and Touqan—break with the erotic tradition of their predecessors, the great Arab poets of earlier periods, but even though the unifying theme is liberation, the reader hears at times the imaginative eloquence of a newer Antar. What a magnificent conceit, for example, is Rashed Hussein's "Letter to a Woman." The poet has been waiting for the girl not yet born, but the train whistle blows and he must run to get on board, but not before leaving a letter in the café near the station with instructions for her when she arrives—Beloved, we just missed each other, by one lifetime!

The major thrust of this poetry, however, has less to do with such lyricism, magnificent as it is, than with the anguish, the rage, and the resolve of an embattled nation. To read this poetry which has grown out of the grief and the fury of an exiled people will be, for many in this country, to experience that sudden shift in perception which the psychologists remind us can occur in simply continuing to observe the same phenomena.

We must, however, confront the issues and the relevant facts squarely here, even though we deal with poetry, especially as we deal with poetry, and particularly this. These are poems which do not seek to comfort; they lack that purpose. Rather to the contrary, they do not permit us to be comfortable. It would be evasive if, in imitation of concern, we focused consideration upon influence and style. This, basically, is a poetry of revolution and like the poetry of the Black revolution, it means to be political, it intends to move people to purpose; it hopes really, as prayer, to change things, to sing—as bullets on a mission, to change men's minds. And so I reflected upon the defining of my own thoughts on the subject.

I, too, watched in a kind of fascinated horror as it became clear during the second World War that the Nazis intended total genocide. At the ghastly spectacle of the ovens of Buchenwald, we were moved from rage to compassion and because of that enormous martyrdom, to sympathy for the restoration of Israel. After the war, as the uncertain struggle in Palestine dragged on, we read Koestler's *Thieves in the Night* and suffered with those valiant, desperate emigrants from Europe in bloody conflict with their dark, vaguely defined but deadly enemy. I was, with Jewish friends, a celebrant in the Lower East Side on the night in 1948 when the state of Israel became a reality and the schoolyard on Rivington Street where I lived exploded with joy. The Solution had proved not final, and a homeland for the victims of Europe's near fatal convulsion was found at last. We were glad.

The Middle East was remote. Moslems, particularly Arabs, were rare in America. There was little enough, with other problems pressing, to cause one even to think about the matter. It was thus troubling and disruptive to begin to discover this had been merely one side of the picture, to become more and more sharply aware of the hundreds of thousands of century-old occupants of the seized land who were wrenched from their homes to join the hopeless communities of the refugee camps, and whose experiences demonstrated once more, if proof were necessary, that the denominator of inflicted pain reaches beyond ethnic and religious boundaries, that Palestinians, also, could suffer under occupation and exile. Mahmoud Darweesh records a dialogue:

> *My ancestors were cremated in Auschwitz.*
> My heart is with them
> Pull out the wires from my skin.
> *And the wounds of yesterday?*
> A shameful scar . . . in the face
>   of the executioner there

I saw, it seemed, a shifting stereotypic image, a wandering mendicant, persecuted and parasitical, preying upon the innocents and absorbing spasmodically their retributive rage, continually the object of their scorn and the subject of his private shame.

There was then the image of an erudite and vastly civilized

prince of fortune, a visage emerging from centuries of persecution with a supreme humanity, with the half smile of all knowledge, all wisdom and of grace, a visage still reflecting, though now rarely, the bearded moral authority of a stern but compassionate Jehovah. I recognized in the latter the awesome Old Testament figure I had met as a boy in the Black church.

There is a new image. After an eternity of humiliation and homelessness, a new David in bright armor has taken the field, with the long lost innocence of command in his eye and control over his destiny in his strong arm. The picture of the ragged outcast of the Western world, the shrewd merchant, facile urbanite, distended intellectual, fades. A champion! The new builders of a nation confident, courageous, whole!

> *Well, boy, what am wrong wid dat?*
> *I was silent for a moment.*
> *Yes, but so it was with our heroes and the winning of the West.*
> *Ah will gives you one and one third second.*
> *For what?*
> *Fo to deal wid* our *heroes.*

But how, then, do I relate to this shifting field? The older, traditional civil rights spokesmen have tended to give a free mandate to the Jewish leadership for the application of their support to the cause of Israel. The younger and more radically-oriented Black leadership has tended to support the Palestinian people and to champion, generally, the new, progressive Moslem governments. Yet, anyone acquainted with the history of the Black struggle in the United States is necessarily aware of how ironic, in one sense, any alignment against Israel might be deemed. The Jewish community has been traditionally a source of support in the long night of the struggle against white bigotry, including the brutal years when the white mobs were rioting in the streets, invading homes, looting and killing in Black communities across the country (producing among other things that most merciless indictment of all:

the Atlanta Litany, when, in Dr. Du Bois' absence, they injured his wife and forced his daughter to hide in the stairwell for safety). Typical of their continuing role, it was the Spingarn brothers and other sympathetic Jews whose assistance was helpful to Du Bois in the launching of the Niagara movement and the founding of the NAACP. Although there may well be a calculated self-interest, as some allege, in a buffer role, there is no gainsaying the long and honorable history of Jewish involvement in the Black man's struggle in America, and, it should be added, in spite of what indefensible practices may prevail at the local furniture store. Except for some misdirected (and generously endowed) voices, the domestic attacks by Blacks upon Jews are less an aspect of Jewish than white identity, and the increasing Black awareness of the colonial pattern (and despite protests that the analogue is not perfect, the colonial category is useful here) of extracting wealth from communities where you do not and will not live, either in corpus or concern. The Jew's own road of adversity has been a long one, and the encounter with him in communities across this land leaves one with the sense that somewhere he is still formulating an equation of his purpose as a people and is in a dialogue with a perhaps re-outfitted but stubborn God.

Is there a different perspective in moving from the purely domestic scene? The competing claims on the issue of Palestine, with their complex historical overlays, are no doubt beyond totally satisfactory solution, and they bear little apparent relation to the Black man's struggle here. There is an evolving aspect, however, under which that issue does relate. Against the disputed merit of the Zionist cause, with which probably most of the listening world sympathized at the time, was the initial misfortune of its imposition under the auspices of a weakening colonial hierarchy. To the extent there is a division on the globe today into those forces tending essentially to preserve the present vastly inequitable organization of world power and those who condemn it as inimical to man's enlightened interest and seek its change, the Black revolution identifies with the latter. To the contrary, Israel appears since its rebirth to have moved closer to the powers of the remodeled colonialism of the West. The Black revolution, especially since Du Bois and Malcolm X, increasingly looks abroad to the internalization of the struggle and ranges itself on the other side. It is significant, also, that Malcolm X was a convert to Islam, that Fanon's revolutionary message was forged in the fire of the struggle of Moslem Algeria, and, farther back, that a Black West Indian immigrant to Africa in the mid-nineteenth century, Edward Blyden, was the author of an influential volume (*Christianity, Islam and the Negro Race*) urging the greater virtue for Black people of Islam over Christianity. We begin to discern the influences which may account, in part certainly, for the strong sympathy towards Islam among today's young Black vanguard. (This is not, of course, the Islam of the oil sheiks who no doubt realize that they must, before long, fold up their privileges and considerately steal away out of there).

There is in this difficult and tortuous labyrinth another facet which impinges. A Semitic people began their hegira in Europe following the Roman destruction of Jerusalem. Two thousand years later, it is in a significant sense a European people who returned, who returned with the science and technologies developed in Europe which has placed them far in advance of their neighbors in the march towards modernization and industrial power. It is suggested, with seeming validity, that the presence in their midst of an ethnically distinct and technologically advanced, though small Western nation, supported by the financial capitals of Europe and America, could seriously disrupt the pace of Arab development and give the Arab states a practically permanent second class status within the orbit of their own area of influence. They, too, now, are going to Europe.

These remarks perhaps, it is true, may have expressed more one side of an issue than the other. The other, however, has been for decades part and parcel of the Western consciousness. In any event, these considerations seemed crucial in shaping an opinion, which is, after all is said, all anyone can account. No issues have been resolved, certainly, nor has the attempt been made. But, more simply, I wanted to set down reflections upon the questions raised by these poets who come from another land but who bear compelling witness to a common humanity.

In view of the strong identification of the younger Black leadership with the Moslem cause, it is significant to note some of the similarities in the poetry of the Palestinian resistance and, mainly, the more recent Black poetry in America. It is striking that the powerful title piece of this volume, "Enemy of the Sun" by Sameeh Al-Qassem, seems to correspond to an earlier period in the Black American poetic experience:

> *You may take the last strip of my land,*
> *Feed my youth to prison cells.*
> *You may plunder my heritage.*
> *You may burn my books, my poems*
> *Or feed my flesh to the dogs.*
> *You may spread a web of terror*
> *On the roofs of my village,*
> *O enemy of the sun,*
> *But*
> *I shall not compromise*
> *And to the last pulse in my veins*
> *I shall resist.*

The similarity is probably no more dramatically seen than in the defiance in the work of Claude McKay, especially in what is practically his title piece, "If We Must Die":

> *If we must die, let it not be like hogs*
> *Hunted and penned in an inglorious spot,*
>
> *While round us bark the mad and hungry dogs,*
> *Making their mock at our accursed lot.*

If we must die, O let us nobly die,
So that our precious blood may not be shed
In vain; then even the monsters we defy
Shall be constrained to honor us though dead!
[. . .]
Like men we'll face the murderous, cowardly pack,
Pressed to the wall, dying, but fighting back!

The Palestinian poet is obviously much conscious of the recent severe military defeat, as McKay was of the uncounted deaths at the hands of the white mobs of the twenties. The mood of the younger Black poets today is less one of defiance before overwhelming odds than one of aggressive challenge to the racists. The problems of racial disability continue apace, but there seems to be emerging among Black youth a kind, almost, of calculated dare to the archetypal "red necked" bigot to continue to inflict on the new generation his long history of racial crimes. Arthur Pfister, in the intentionally unvarnished language of the Black masses so characteristic of the new Black writing, warns of the danger for a Southern white man to be found upon a country road in Alabama:

> .... *when we came upon—*
> *a* craker
> MAY DE LAW-AW-AW-AW-AW-AW-AW-AW-AW-
> AWD HELP HIM!!!!

Both lines of poetry contain scornful reference to the older traditions of their people which have left them defenseless before their enemies. "Anti-Aircraft Amulets" by Al-Qassem is a moving, ironic, and withering indictment of a useless, superstition-ridden past, which merits quoting at some length:

> *I was a child of nine*
> *Then*
> *I sucked the milk of tragedy*

I was a child with dreamy eyes,
Thousands of nets surrounded me
On that day
I remember
Mother's troubled voice:
"Tonight
When you go to bed,
Sleep in your clothes
And don't take your shoes off!"
I did not understand what she meant then,
Yet—I cried.

It is nightfall
The semi-circle of the murdered moon,
cries in the street
And my father has not yet returned
The rumors speak of betrayals
By the high command
Of the soldiers' thrust—Backward
We cried.

[...]

People of Ramah
The conqueror has arrived
Why sing songs of glory?
Aim all your amulets at the aircraft
Call for God's wrath
Throw the Commandments.
Al-Jifr
And all holy verses of heaven.

I was a child then—
they taught me that
The affairs of earth

Are in the hands of heaven
[...]
They taught me to obey the prophets
Without asking,
Who are they?
And what have they done for the wretched?
They taught me to dance on a rope,
To humble women
To believe in witchcraft
To fear the nightfall!
[...]

Defeated father—humbled mother
To Hell with
My inheritance of tribal teachings,
My savage rites.
I cut the stupid customs
From the roots
I spit my hate
My shame
Into the faces of the devout
The holy ones
I kick the garbage of my defeat and
My humility
Into the face of the dervishes—
The barking half-men—the office holders

From the depth of my Hell
My voice prevails:
I condemn you to death
You,
The mud stuck on the sole of my
Great history,

More briefly, in contrast, and in a more homely vein, are
Charles Anderson's lines:

I've been prayin' for centuries
To some God up in the sky.

God said, G 'way boy
I don't want to hear you cry,
But I know Jesus heard me
Cause he spit right in my eye.

And Don Lee's famous:

> *Jesus saves,*
> *Jesus saves,*
> *Jesus saves-S&H Green Stamps.*

Don Lee, who met some of the Arab poets at the Pan-African cultural festival in Algiers in the summer of 1969, is a literary figure whose historical importance is not yet fully recognized. He is the first Black writer in America to achieve a national reputation without being filtered through the editorial screen of the white psyche, one problem the Palestinian poets have not had to face, at least, hopefully, to the same degree. Lee titled probably his most famous volume *Don't Cry, Scream*. This is the message of both traditions. The time for weeping is over; lamentation is for the elders, mothers. The Palestinian poet, Mahmoud Darweesh, asks:

What is the use if I weep
What storm will be crushed by my tears.

And Al-Qassem, after the defeat of June 5, 1967:

I do not weep, I do not smile.

The struggle is all demanding so that poetry, itself, seems irrelevant unless it can serve the cause. Nizar Qabbani confesses his overnight change:

From a poet of love and longing
To one who writes with a knife

and he urges:

oh, poetry, be angry
oh prose, be bitter
oh mind, be rebellious
lest we all become a flock of refugees.

For Imamu Ameer Baraka (LeRoi Jones), the poem is useless
unless it is a weapon:

We want "poems that kill."
Assassin poems, Poems that shoot
guns.

And Qabbani says:

The flute and the lute
Do not secure victory

Our extemporaneous ways
Brought us fifty thousand new tents

But Ameer Baraka is the author of *Blues People,* and here in the
United States where cultural nationalism is strong, the Black artist
prides himself upon his gift of spontaneity; although he, too, has
concluded it is not enough, Baraka calls for "Poems that wrestle
cops into alleys." "Put it on him, poem," he says of the "negro-
leader," supine and "negotiating" in the White House.

There is a difference in emphasis noticeable in the two bodies
of poetry. In the Palestinian poetry there is not only the fiercest
determination to resist, but the most rigorous and unsparing self
criticism, i.e., of the traditional Arab society. Rashed Hussein in

"The Horses" condemns the disastrous Arabian glorification of the male hero as a thoroughbred stallion, while all around, ignorance, disease, and poverty prevail. But there is not only condemnation of the old ways, but also strong emphasis upon the necessity of acquiring the scientific and technological knowledge essential to modern power. There is a means test not only for financial aid, but also for revolution!

There does not appear to be an equivalent insistence upon such a preparatory phase by the Black poet in America. The revolutionary *élan* is there, but not, to the same degree, an explicit concern with means, although Gaston Neal does reflect such an awareness: "the slow tedious math of power will begin to creep into our shoulders."

The poetry in this volume, it is soon clear, insists upon the rejection of an aesthetically purist approach; it compels us to confront squarely the issue of liberation. It is basically, then, a poetry of revolution and, like the poetry of the Black revolution, it means to be political; as poetry, yes it sings—as bullets on a mission; it calls for change.

> *By the rivers of Babylon, there we sat down, yea we wept,*
> *   when we remembered Zion.*
> *We hanged our harps upon the willows in the midst thereof.*
> *For there they that carried us away captive required of us a*
> *   song; and they that wasted us required of us mirth, saying,*
> *   Sing us one of the songs of Zion.*
> *How shall we sing the Lord's song in a strange land?*
> *If I forget thee, O Jerusalem, let my right hand forget her*
> *   cunning.*

For anyone shaped under the influence of the Judeo Greco tradition, it is troublesome even to consider qualification of the imperative of those lines. Yet the poets in this collection are eloquent witnesses to an opposed moral claim, validated by centuries of possession with their intangible skeins of memory. Conflicting claims have for centuries been the hallmark of the Crescent; never have the consequences been so potentially disastrous. Perhaps the poets may help to illuminate this fury and find a path to avoid the holocaust. Al-Qassem perceives and explores in "In Enemy Lines" the cruel paradoxes of our animosities. He condemns anti-semitism and the Fascist threat:

> *Down with the shame of man*
> *Raised by the Fascists waving mud-stained banners*
> *Those words that say:*
> No dogs, Jews, or Negroes allowed.

Is there a beginning here?

> *Who knows where the stars stand*
> *in the creator's order of glory.*

wrote Nelly Sachs:

> *And where peace begins*
> *and if in the tragedy of earth*
> *the torn bloody gill of the fish*
> *is intended*
> *to supplement with its ruby red*
> *the constellation of Torment,*
> *to write the first letter*
> *of the wordless language –*

> *True, love has the look*
> *which strikes through bones like lightning*

For a moment she seems to hope against hope in the power of love, but she moves to her central perception having little to do with the triumph or folly of this world except for the meaning of survival through extinction and metamorphosis.

But the poet from Palestine now must move to this same aware-
ness. Al-Qassem, too, probes the far reaches of the spirit, death,
and the resurrection, as he writes in "Job's Diary":

For centuries
It was said
That there are winds
That there are pellets
And there is—it is told
A seed
Germinating a soul into the rock
Opening a road to the sun.
What if I stab my dagger
Into the seed, the rock, and the sun?
It is said that there are winds
And pellets
And roots
That despair does not blight!

We can only stand with bowed heads, finally, in silence, before
the passion of Sameeh Al-Qassem:

I walk.
Straight as a ramrod
Head high
I walk.
An olive branch
And a dove
In my palm
And on my shoulders my coffin
And I walk.
My heart a red moon,
My heart a garden;
My lips a rainy sky,
At times

Love
And I walk—walk!
Straight as a ramrod
Head high
An olive branch
And a dove
In my palm
And on my shoulder
My coffin.

SAMUEL W. ALLEN
Tuskegee, Alabama
1970

INTRODUCTION TO
THE 2025 EDITION

From the dust-laden streets of besieged Gaza to the ancient olive groves of the West Bank, Palestinian poets infuse their verses with the resilience of their ancestors and the weight of their enduring struggles. Despite attempts to silence them, their voices persist and resonate with the cries of oppressed communities worldwide. In an environment rife with violence and censorship, writing emerges as an act of defiance—a manifestation of autonomy and dignity that strikes a profound chord with people everywhere.

This collection explores Palestinian resistance poetry, acknowledging these works as both personal expressions and essential threads in the global tapestry of resistance to oppression. These poems are primarily written by Palestinian poets from the 1960s to the present, most of whom lived under Israeli rule, a small number living in other parts of the world. It includes as well poems by Arab poets committed to the Palestinian cause. Each poem serves as a testament to a history that resists erasure and a future that demands liberation. Through their words, these poets illuminate the ongoing struggle for justice, reminding us that the quest for freedom knows no borders and unites all who seek liberation.

In the areas that border Palestine, i.e., Syria, Lebanon, Jordan, and Egypt, as well as other places in the Arab world, poetry was shaped by the neo-classical Arab revival led by Lebanese scholars such as Butrus al-Bustani, Naseef al-Yaziji, and

Ahmed Faris al-Chidyaq. This movement which produced poets, teachers, historians, journalists, and novelists started in Lebanon and Syria and shared in the cultural development of Egypt, Iraq, Palestine, and other Arab countries. Over time, the nature of the poems began to change in dramatic ways; increasingly, they incorporated religious, political, and historical issues and showed the influence of the pre- and post-Islamic literary and cultural contributions as well as influence from the Bible and Mesopotamian and pharaonic civilizations, and the European renaissance. Arabic literary societies thrived with the rise of an Arabic language press in South and North America. These Mahjar societies, such as al-Usbah al-Andalusiyah (The Andalusian Band) in Brazil and al-Rabitah al-Qalamiyah (The Pen League) in New York, influenced new generations of poets and writers across the Arab world, including Palestinian poets and writers. This was seen in the work of poets Mahmoud Darweesh, Sameeh Al-Qassem, and many others.

For Arabs, poetry has long held a sense of magic. The ancient Arabs of the pre-Islamic period regarded poets not only as defenders against insults to their community, and as glorifiers and preservers of its deeds, but also as individuals endowed with supernatural abilities. Contemporary poets like Kahlil Gibran view the poet as someone "gifted with a vision that penetrates hidden metaphysical realities that surpass logical reasoning and tangible experience."* Such insight is seen as "relevant and indispensable" for true progress and manifests through symbols that express personal, national, and universal meanings.

While poetry often speaks directly to its community, it also transcends boundaries, acting as an international language with universal messages. It is increasingly vital that poets are understood and appreciated beyond their immediate contexts.

---

* From a letter written by Kahlil Gibran to Andrew Ghareeb, translator of Gibran's Arabic works into English, 1928.

According to the late poet and activist Audre Lorde, poetry is not a luxury. "It is a vital necessity of our existence. It forms the quality of the light within which we predicate our hopes and dreams toward survival and change, first made into language, then into idea, then into more tangible action. Poetry is the way we help give name to the nameless so it can be thought. The farthest horizons of our hopes and fears are cobbled by our poems, carved from the rock experiences of our daily lives." Despite the richness of Arabic poetry, only a limited amount of works by revolutionary contemporary poets have been translated into English.

This is ironic, considering many poets—especially those writing in free verse rather than traditional qasidah—have drawn inspiration from both Western poets and Arab expatriates who have settled in the United States. They were the pioneers of free verse poetry, with some later evolving their own distinct styles. The diverse array of poems in this anthology encapsulates a spectrum of emotions, including introspection, self-reflection, joy, determination, suffering, anger, and solidarity with all who have endured colonial oppression, creating a remarkable and rich panorama of both individuals and their communities.

Palestinian poets have utilized their poetry to articulate the pain of displacement and the pressing need for self-determination. Under occupation, literature transcends mere art—it transforms into a weapon of resistance. Their works are a testament to the devastation brought by the Nakba, when over 750,000 Palestinians were exiled from their homes, villages, and towns, with only about 150,000 remaining under Israeli Occupation and military rule. Through their verses, they confront prevailing Western narratives, ensuring that Palestinian history and identity are recognized on their own terms, giving voice to the agony and resilience of their people. The launching of numerous attempted and actualized coups was, in part, a response to the 1948 defeat and the widespread suffering of the Palestinian people. Among these was the first coup in Syria in 1949, and, more importantly, the Egyptian Revolution of 1952, which inspired the overthrow of several governments in the Arab World. The Arab uprisings infused hope into the hearts of Palestinians, galvanizing aspirations for return and renewal. The 1956 war, in which Israel, Britain, and France launched an attack against Egypt, further bolstered those sentiments.

During this period, Palestinian poets not only represented the struggles of their own people and the Arab nations, but also the plight of all oppressed communities. The events had given rise to a new type of poetry, characterized by the experience of the refugee. Poets of the 1940s and '50s began to explore the enduring refugee pain of hunger, displacement, and alienation as they yearned for return. Their words echoed a demand for social justice, liberation, and progress. This sector of the Palestinian populace draws metaphorical strength from roots deeply embedded in love for their land, like the olive and orange groves that form an integral part of their identity.

Palestine represents a great, immeasurable beauty. Singers, most notably, have paid countless tributes to this land. Fairuz, a Lebanese singer, known among other titles as the Soul of the Arab World, has sung moving songs with her enchanting voice. Her words are not only poetic, but they are also a culmination of prayers, the raw expression of every Arab, every human being devoted to justice. In "Zahrat Al Mada'in," Fairuz sings of Jerusalem as the flower of all cities; she points to Jerusalem's temples, churches, and mosques, to the weeping faces of *Maryam* (Mary) and her son, to those who were exiled and martyred at the gates, and to the homeless children of the land. Fayrouz also describes the tireless longing of the refugees who dream of return as the nightingales fly freely over the border in *Sanarja'a Yawman* (We will return one day).

Poetry in Palestinian culture has long been considered a treasured and potent art form. By the late nineteenth century, with the emergence of a Palestinian national consciousness, poetry began to assume a distinctly political tone. It became a medium for articulating opposition to Ottoman rule and advocating for

Palestinian independence, reflecting the evolving social and political landscape. During pivotal moments of Palestinian resistance, such as the 1936–1939 Arab Revolt and the 1948 Nakba, poetry served as an essential tool of political defiance. Extending beyond the written word, it was often performed before large, passionate audiences, functioning as a rallying cry for the poor and marginalized. Poets like Ibrahim Touqan and Abu Salma exemplified this movement. Their work actively engaged with and inspired their Palestinian audience, igniting national pride, reminding people of their identity, and asserting their sense of belonging. Even the simplest verses could evoke profound emotions.

In contrast, Palestinian poetry following the 1967 War diverged significantly from the literature prevailing in the broader Arab world, where feelings of hopelessness and defeat characterized many works. The Israeli occupation of the Palestinian territories and the dislocation of Palestinians ushered in a new form of Palestinian revolutionary poetry. This shift occurred not only in areas that have been under Israeli control since 1948 and those captured in 1967, but also among the Palestinian diaspora. Poets such as Mahmoud Darweesh, Tawfiq Zayyad, and Fadwa Touqan began to write a new form of poetry in the aftermath of the June 1967 defeat, symbolizing hope and resilience amid a poetic landscape marked by despair. These poets connected deeply with their people and their struggles, helping to articulate a narrative of hope.

Darweesh famously spoke of "lost innocence," reflecting on how his childhood marked the onset of both personal and national tragedy. His work emphasized a deeper form of resistance that transcended simple emotional rejection and physical defiance. This concept of *sumūd*, or steadfastness, captures the essence of a profound revolution—one rooted in education and empowerment.[*]

The writer, journalist, editor, and member of the Popular

---

[*] Mohammed Sawaie, *The Tent Generations: Palestinian Poems* (Banipal Books, 2023), 18.

Front for the Liberation of Palestine (PFLP), Ghassan Kanafani, is considered the father of the genre *Adab Al-Muqawama*, or Resistance Literature. Kanafani was assassinated in 1972 in Beirut. During the 1950s and '60s, cultural genres blossomed, fostering solidarity with other colonized peoples and Arab kinships through literature. This era also gave rise to another significant term: *Al-'iltizam*, meaning "the commitment," which refers to the dedication to leverage literature as a platform to raise national issues and to confront aggression.[*]

Many Palestinian poets, especially Darweesh, Touqan, and Al-Qassem, drew strength from both natural and mythical symbols, identifying deeply with the land they had lost. Natural symbols like trees and mountains reinforced their connection to their homeland, while mythical and spiritual symbols spanned both local and distant sources. The recurrence of Christ and the crucifixion is notable in their work. Moreover, Sakhr Sayf used the story of Samson and Delilah, Mai Sayegh used Al Khansā, Yusuf Al Khateeb used Eleazar, Muin Boseiso used the story of Jonah and the whale, and Khalid Abu Khalid Antarah returned to the use of heritage and its symbols to describe the struggle that the Palestinian people were going through.[**]

Palestinian poetry, during this period, often utilized symbolism as a means of expressing the Palestinian cause, resisting regulations that prohibited even the mention of the word "Palestine"; as, for example, in the use of the olive tree as a powerful symbol of national identity or the martyr, who represented struggle and sacrifice. The *fallahin*, or peasants, had become central figures in poetry, embodying their earlier struggle against land appropriation and the tyranny of feudal lords. Samy Hadawi, a Palestinian historian, said that peasants are "attached to the soil, perhaps more than any other people. To the Arab peasant, the land is the sole means of his sustenance, the root of his family life, his culture and

---

[*] Sawaie, 15.
[**] *Mawsuah Al Filastiniyah* 4, (Beirut, 1990): 38–44.

identification with his family mores."* Thus, the poetry of those who remained in Palestine post–1967 narrates the epic saga of a people defending their roots and identity against annihilation. It also recounts the Palestinian individual's quest for survival and the right to live freely on their own land, affirming their humanity. This body of work represents a staunch declaration of identity against relentless efforts to erase it; Palestinians refuse to become refugees twice, choosing instead to remain in their homeland, even when treated as second-class citizens. Their unique experience as a minority in their own land symbolizes both rebirth and a replanting of themselves.

The image of the "transient Palestinian" is also a prevalent one. In her article "The Alienation of Palestine in Palestinian Poetry" for the Winter 1981 issue of the *Arab Studies Quarterly*, Jacqueline Ismael points to how rootlessness symbolizes alienation. Palestinians become "human[s] without a home, a people without a homeland, a past without a future, and a present without a past."** This alienation also implies a loss of the sensory experiences often celebrated in poetry, such as touch and smell. This painful reality resonates throughout their poetic expressions.

For those poets who were forced into exile, their subject matter remained consistent, echoing themes of sorrow over Arab failures and lamenting a bleak present while expressing concern for the future. They critiqued Palestinian leaders and foreign governments for betraying their country, selling their land, capitulating to external powers.

Some poets, like Abu Salma, vehemently rejected this betrayal in their works—expressing frustration over leaders who were both enemies and friends. He contended that these leaders traded in Palestine's name while simultaneously accusing

---

* James Zogby, "Palestinian Identity and the Land of Palestine," *Freedom Ways* 23, no. 2 (1983): 120.
** Jacqueline S. Ismael, "The Alienation of Palestine in Palestinian Poetry," *Arab Studies Quarterly* 3, no. 1 (1981): 47.

Palestinian people of betrayal. Poets in exile began to emphasize a sense of loss, as captured poignantly in the lines of Muhammad al-Qaisi: "I pull the aged jars of sorrow from my soul, inherited tortures along my eyelids . . . I cannot forget the eyes of strangers in exile, slapping me as they ask what is your identity. Yes, I am Palestinian."*

Abdul Rahim Omar explored feelings of persecution in his work, even as other poets seemingly took pride in their torment. He proclaimed that the era of heroism had passed and expressed his disillusionment through the poetry of Abu Zayd Al Hilali, Antarah ibn Shaddad, and Al Zeer Salem, three major heroic figures from Arab folklore who defended their tribes and lamented the loss of valor and tradition.

Nonetheless, some poets began to focus on the emergence of a new leadership. Inspired by Gamal Abdel Nasser's calls for Arab unity and identity, many regarded him as a potential savior, especially following the nationalization of the Suez Canal, the 1956 War, and the unification of Egypt and Syria. They discovered a renewed sense of Arab identity that complemented their Palestinian one, though setbacks arising from the collapse of this unity and disappointments over the Iraqi revolution in 1958 later tempered their expectations. Poets like Kamal Nasser articulated these sentiments, recounting the story of a crucified people left to wander for years but who nonetheless resisted and united in the face of adversity, giving rise to a new light amidst the darkness—a testament to the resilience of their spirit.**

The poets who wrote during the British Mandate period criticized the Palestinian and Arab leaders they blamed for the loss of Palestine. The perspectives which criticized some Arab governments, and at the same time embraced Nasser during the 1950s and '60s, reflected the diverse views of Palestinian and Arab poets. These were discussed in two important articles published

---

* *Mawsuah Al Filastiniyah* 4 (Beirut, 1990): 13, 14.
** *Mawsuah Al Filastiniyah*, 298.

in the *Mawsuah Al Filastiniyah* (The Palestinian Encyclopedia): "Poetry in Palestine Up to 1967" by Professor Ihsan Abbas*, and "Contemporary Palestinian Poetry" by Professor Mahmoud Chraih.**

New poets also flourished in exile, drawing inspiration from contemporary poetic movements, particularly Iraqi poets like Nazik al-Malaika, Badr Shakir al-Sayyab, and Abdul Wahab Al-Bayyaty. Their work reflected these influences but also departed from them. Following the second wave of displacement during the Naksa of 1967, a new poetic form surfaced, characterized by an emphasis on sacrifice and martyrdom, reflecting the evolving landscape of Palestinian identity and resistance amid growing challenges.

Some Palestinian poets who remained in Israel were initially influenced by Mahjar poets from North and South America, leading to the emergence of a new prose poetry style that synthesized traditional themes with influences from American, European, and Asian literary traditions. This trend was mirrored in countries such as Lebanon, Egypt, Syria, and Iraq, where poets like Khalil Hawi, Badr Shakir al-Sayyab, Abdul Wahab Al-Bayyaty, and Ahmad Dahbour also inspired emerging Palestinian poets.

The new Palestinian poetry challenged the traditional Arab poetic conventions, primarily in their adoption of free verse that deviated from the thematic confines of the traditional qasidah. It drew inspiration from the emerging Arab poetic movement, as well as from Frantz Fanon, whose writing on anti-colonial struggle resonated with the Palestinian cause. They expressed solidarity with Black Americans and Native Americans who endured similar kinds of oppression. Tawfiq Zayyad, the late mayor of Nazareth, sent a greeting and solidarity message to Native Americans in the early 1980s: "The future belongs to equality and brotherhood—

---

* *Mawsuah Al Filastiniyah*, 19–26.
** *Mawsuah Al Filastiniyah*, 40–47.

and we the oppressed people who struggle against injustice are the people who will make this future a reality *for all the people.*[*] Despite the risks of imprisonment and house arrest faced by those who wrote in this new style, poets such as Mahmoud Darweesh, Tawfiq Zayyad, and Sameeh Al-Qassem preserved their national identity and commitment to their cause, as reflected in Zayyad's poem "We Shall Remain."

Ironically, many of these poems, particularly those by Darweesh and Al-Qassem, contain significant biblical imagery, reflecting a profound sense of uprootedness and a longing for the promised land. Al-Qassem's "Job's Diary" invokes the Hebrew prophet Isaiah for justice to illustrate the growing impatience of the Palestinian diaspora. This narrative, though relatively unknown, highlights the connections between the Palestinian experience and the oppression faced by Black Americans, Africans under colonial occupation, and oppressed people in Asia and Latin America, illustrating the solidarity in human suffering, regardless of geography.

Writing in a neoclassical style, Haroun Hashem Rashid infuses his words with an intensity reminiscent of brimstone, declaring:

> *I will not live as a homeless person.*
> *I will not remain handcuffed.*
> *I am a great revolution,*
> *which will bring storms and death.*

Tawfiq Sayegh, on the other hand, approaches the theme of exile from a deeply personal perspective, speaking to his love, his God, and his homeland:

> *You are the ones who have sentenced me to exile,*
> *and made me settle in exile.*

---

* Zogby, "Palestinian Identity," 125.

My life becomes constant torture.
Every new night, I am pursued, tried, tortured, and led to
the guillotine.
Every new morn, I am hunted.

Another notable poet and novelist, Jabra Ibrahim Jabra, also drew on themes of exile and alienation to express the disorientation caused by living in a foreign land:

Our land, homeland
Remember us as we roam aimless
Between the thorns of different deserts and landscapes.

In addition to Palestinian poets who took up the Palestinian struggle, many contemporary Arab poets began to reflect on this pressing issue in their work as well. The new Arab poetry emerged alongside the Palestinian question, with many emphasizing the suffering of Palestinian refugees and those under occupation. This concern was notably present in the poetry of Syrian poet Muhammad Al Maghout, whose "Ghabat Yaffa" (The Yaffa Forest) was published in 1953, and Egyptian poet Salah Abdel Sabour, who addressed the invasion of the Tatars in 1954. Iraqi poet Badr Shakir Al Sayyab also captured the essence of loss in "The Caravan of Loss" (1956). In the early 1960s, Abdul Wahab Al-Bayyaty employed the figure of Sinbad as a metaphor for the Palestinian experience of exile and displacement:

I am Sinbad,
I am like a gypsy in the hearts of your youth.
I am Sinbad as a sad beggar.
The ants eat his flesh and the birds of prey eat his ears.

Lebanese poet Khalil Hawi articulated the tragedy of the Arab nation's failure to address the Palestinian cause, through the figure of Eleazar, who, though revived by Jesus, remained paralyzed, representing the Arab inability to respond to Palestine.

Professor Samuel Allen states that this poetry "basically, is a poetry of revolution and like the poetry of the Black revolution, it means to be political, it intends to move people to purpose; it hopes really, as prayer, to change things, to sing—as bullets on a mission, to change men's minds." This comparison emphasizes how words can serve as weapons against oppression. These poems resonated with their Palestinian audience, awakening the national spirit and reminding them of their identity, heritage, and cause. In many respects, they are human cries that underscore how many people around the world continue to fight for liberation.

These themes resonate throughout contemporary Palestinian poetry, reinforcing the essence of resistance as a blend of hope and defiance. For these poets, experiences of oppression, suffering, freedom, and resistance are everyday realities to which they respond and give shape to with a dynamic form of poetry.

The Nakba of 1948 and the subsequent 1967 defeat remain subjects of historical debate. Various factors contributed to these events, ultimately resulting in the expulsion and displacement of hundreds of thousands of Palestinians and the fall of numerous Palestinian cities. The massacres, including that of Kafr Qasim on October 29, 1956, during which Israeli border police murdered forty-nine innocent Palestinians, among them women and children, left the Palestinian community in shock.

As these atrocities continued, hope for a quick return to homes and towns faded as the ambitions of the Zionist Congress, spearheaded by Theodor Herzl, sought to seize Palestinian land. Israeli Prime Minister David Ben-Gurion openly stated the need to "expel the Arabs and take their place."* After facing Ottoman and British rule, Palestinians found themselves once again facing colonization.

---

* "JPS responds to CAMERA's call for accuracy: Ben Gurion and the Arab Transfer," *Journal of Palestine Studies* 41, no. 2 (2012): 245-250.

****

My collaboration on the translation of *Enemy of the Sun*, first published in 1970, opened my eyes to the profound connections between the struggles of Palestinians and Black Americans, both shaped by a shared history of racial and colonial injustice. During the Civil Rights Movement of the 1960s, the Student Nonviolent Coordinating Committee (SNCC) was among the first organizations to publicly support Palestinian rights. Despite facing funding cuts in retaliation for their stance, they remained steadfast. This solidarity was crucial in linking the Black and Palestinian struggles.

Key figures in this connection included Stokely Carmichael, who later changed his name to Kwame Ture, a pivotal leader in the US Black liberation struggle and the broader African liberation movement. Serving as the "honorary prime minister" of the Black Panther Party and later leading the Pan-African People's Revolutionary Party, Ture championed the notion that the fight for justice transcended borders. I had the opportunity to meet him in Iraq in 1976 and later in the United States.

During my college years, I co-founded a student magazine with a friend and translated Palestinian poetry, including Sameeh Al-Qassem's "Enemy of the Sun." I traveled as a reporter for Collegiate Press Service and *The Torch* to the Middle East in 1969, where I interviewed Fatah/PLO leader Yasser Arafat. Just before my departure, a friend invited me to attend a poetry reading featuring Palestinian poets, most of whom still lived under Israeli rule. I attended the event, where poets from both Jordan and the Occupied Territories shared their verses. Upon returning to the US, I translated the work of several poets, including Mahmoud Darweesh, Sameeh Al-Qassem, and Tawfiq Zayyad, which were subsequently published in student magazines and newspapers.

Around the same period, Naseer Aruri, a professor and activist, was also translating Palestinian poetry. Naseer—who taught political science at the University of Massachusetts and became president of the Association of Arab American University Graduates—proposed that we collaborate and bring together our translations for a book of Palestinian poetry.

Though finding a publisher was initially challenging, eventually Drum & Spear Press, known for its dedication to African and African American literature, agreed to publish the book. Although the book gained traction in academic circles, it largely eluded mainstream attention. Nonetheless, it became a critical text for activists and intellectuals. As the first anthology of Palestinian poetry published in the United States, it played a seminal role in introducing these works to new audiences and spurred further translations into various languages. Charlie Cobb, a leader and founder of Drum & Spear, said, "[*Enemy of the Sun*] was arguably the best book we published, in terms of quality, the actual physical quality of the publication, and the quality of the poetry."*

Translated Palestinian poetry acts as a conduit connecting diverse audiences to the lived realities of Palestinians, while simultaneously challenging dominant Western narratives. More than mere linguistic conversion, translation seeks to preserve the essence of the original poem—embedding themes of exile, longing, and resistance within a broader global literary discourse.

However, translation presents its own challenges; the task of capturing emotional depth, cultural nuances, and sensory details—from the scent of jasmine to the taste of olives—requires a delicate balance of fidelity to the source and accessibility for the reader. Kahlil Gibran famously noted that translating Arabic is more difficult than writing in it, emphasizing that translation itself is an art form. The challenge intensifies when transitioning between Arabic and English. Despite these hurdles, translated Palestinian poetry serves as a form of literary diplomacy, promoting cross-cultural understanding and providing a counter-

---

* Charlie Cobb, "Charlie Cobb Interview, re post-SNCC activities," interview by Joshua Clark Davis, *Civil Rights Movement Archive*, October 16, 2015, audio 52:01, https://www.crmvet.org/nars/cobb2015.pdf.

narrative to prevailing portrayals of the Palestinian struggle.

Just a few years after its initial release, *Enemy of the Sun* sold out, and with the closure of Drum & Spear Press, the book fell out of print. Recently, there has been a resurgence of interest in the book, with scholars, students, and pro-Palestinian activists frequently citing the resistance poets included in the anthology and many calling for the publication of a new edition of this important work. It has been featured in student groups and adopted at some universities as part of their coursework, ensuring the continuation of its legacy.

The rising demand for the original edition and a new publication arose partly due to connections with George Jackson, the Black Panther leader who was killed in prison in 1971. The shared experience of oppression resonated deeply with both Palestinians and African Americans, a synergy reflected in Sameeh Al-Qassem's verses:

> *You may build walls of hatred around me.*
> *You may glue my eyes to humiliations.*
> O enemy of the sun,
> *But*
> *I shall not compromise,*
> *And to the last pulse in my veins*
> *I shall resist.*

Imprisoned at eighteen for theft, Jackson spent eleven years in prison, including seven years in solitary confinement. Over time, he evolved into a revolutionary thinker, articulating radical perspectives on race, class, and resistance. His works, particularly *Soledad Brother* and *Blood in My Eye*, continue to inspire liberation movements globally. His tragic death only heightened his influence, demonstrating his solidarity with the Palestinian cause. Jackson recognized that the fights for justice in Palestine and the United States were deeply interconnected. He urged the Black Panther Party to issue multiple statements of solidarity with the

Palestinian struggle, believing that genuine liberation necessitated self-determination and unity among oppressed peoples.

In the wake of Jackson's death, among his personal effects was a handwritten document titled "Enemy of the Sun," which was later published in the Black Panther Newspaper under his name. Professor Greg Thomas was one of the first people to discover that the poems "Enemy of the Sun" and "I Defy," long attributed to Jackson, were in fact from Naseer Aruri's and my book *Enemy of the Sun*. Professor Thomas reached out to me while he was writing an article about the bonds between Palestinians and Black Americans. He also organized several exhibits in the US and Palestine about Jackson's connection to Al-Qassem. Jackson's tenacious resistance against systemic racism highlights the interconnectedness of various oppressions—an enduring theme echoed in Al-Qassem's powerful poetry. Both men channeled their personal suffering into a clarion call for justice, challenging the status quo and advocating for global solidarity. Thomas further enriched this new edition with a new foreword.

Scholars such as Daphne Muse have noted the shared experiences of racial discrimination faced by both Black Americans and Palestinians. Muse asserts, "There is a clear parallel between Black Americans and Palestinians." She also highlights the similarities between Indigenous struggles in the US, apartheid South Africa, and the occupation in Palestine.

This intersection of Palestinian and Black American struggles reveals an often-overlooked but crucial function of poetry: its ability to transcend borders, fostering connections between people who share a collective pain and a commitment to resistance. The words of both Sameeh Al-Qassem and Jackson serve as reminders that human suffering is a shared experience that unites all those who fight for justice.

The solidarity between Palestinian and Black activists worldwide is poignantly captured in the words of Black feminist poet June Jordan. In 1996, after visiting Palestinian refugee camps in Lebanon, she declared, "I was born a Black woman / and now / I am become a Palestinian." This profound statement underscores the deep connections between these two struggles—both rooted in racial oppression and national dispossession. Jordan's words are a reminder of the powerful links between liberatory movements across the globe.

This international solidarity also extends to the Black liberation movement through influential figures like Malcolm X, who drew explicit connections between the oppression faced by Black Americans and Palestinians. In his speeches, he emphasized the importance of self-determination for all oppressed peoples, including Palestinians. His advocacy for Palestinian rights broadened the civil rights movement's focus, establishing a global framework for justice that transcended national boundaries.

The global resonance of the Palestinian struggle even reached Asia, where Rabindranath Tagore, the eminent Indian poet and philosopher, expressed solidarity with the Palestinian people's cause. His poem "Where the Mind Is Without Fear" speaks to a universal yearning for freedom, a sentiment that echoes among Palestinians and others fighting for independence worldwide. Mahatma Gandhi, a key figure in India's independence movement, similarly admired the Palestinian struggle, recognizing it as a part of a broader global fight for self-determination.

The principles of Pan-Africanism align closely with the themes present in Palestinian poetry, as both movements emphasize unity and resistance against oppression. Influential figures in Pan-Africanism—including Maya Angelou, Léopold Sédar Senghor, and Aimé Césaire—found kinship with Palestinian poets in their shared pursuit of dignity, autonomy, and justice.

Furthermore, the poetic bonds linking Palestinian and South African poets form a rich tapestry of shared struggle, resilience, and defiance. Both nations have suffered the brutality of colonization and oppression, shaped by the enduring legacies of European imperialism, and their poets have wielded verse as a weapon against these forces. Though the scars of colonialism run deep—Palestinians endured British colonial rule followed by Israeli occupation, and South Africans suffered systemic racial segregation under apartheid—both movements persist in their quest for liberation and justice.

Much like their South African, Black, and Indigenous counterparts, Palestinian poets have used their voices to challenge oppression and articulate their longing for a homeland free from foreign control. The themes of resistance in Palestinian and South African poetry are strikingly similar. The poetry emerging from the Soweto Uprising in the 1960s and '70s, for instance, was a powerful testament to the spirit of defiance, as poets like Mongane Wally Serote captured the urgent desire for liberation.

In this broader poetic symphony of resistance, Palestinian and South African poets harmonize in a shared melody of defiance and hope. Their words, flowing like rivers of ink, carry the weight of history while igniting the promise of a world where freedom and justice reign. Each line penned becomes a call to action, each metaphor a plea for liberation—a testament to poetry's enduring power to unite peoples and movements across time and space. Palestinian poets offer a unifying perspective on the struggle for freedom and human rights, standing in opposition to those who seek to obliterate their history, culture, and identity.

To this day, the ties of Black-Palestinian solidarity remain strong. Black internationalism, as defined by Noura Erakat and Marc Lamont Hill in the *Journal of Palestine Studies*, reflects a twenty-first-century movement among Black Americans who seek to contextualize their fight for freedom in the US as part of a global struggle against transnational systems of racial capitalism.* Palestinians in Gaza were under assault from a brutal Israeli military campaign known as "Operation Protective

---

* Noura Erakat and Marc Lamont Hill, "Black-Palestinian Transnational Solidarity: Renewals, Returns, and Practice," *Journal of Palestine Studies* 48, no. 4 (August 1, 2019): 7-16.

Edge," while those in the West Bank faced regular incursions by occupying forces. In this moment of convergence, Palestinians utilized social media to share strategies for self-protection against tear gas, while Black activists began donning keffiyehs at protests. This fusion of grassroots solidarity birthed a joint struggle uniting Black Americans and Palestinians against oppression.

For the past two years, the eyes of the world have been fixated on Palestine. An incursion by Palestinian fighters aimed at capturing Israeli hostages to negotiate the release of hundreds of Palestinians held in the Occupied Territories led to an explosive and brutal military campaign against the people of Gaza. A record number of children have been orphaned, killed, and suffered severe injuries, while more journalists have been killed in this specific period than in any previous conflict in the history of the world. As of April 22, 2025, preliminary investigations by the Committee to Protect Journalists (CPJ) revealed that at least 176 journalists and media workers have lost their lives. Major human rights organizations have overwhelmingly recognized that the Israeli government is carrying out genocide against the Palestinians.

Notably, South Africa has brought a case against Israel to the International Criminal Court, claiming that the Israeli government is deliberately committing genocide against the Palestinian people. The Court acknowledged South Africa's arguments and issued provisional measures ordering Israel to refrain from any actions contrary to the 1948 Genocide Convention, although it stopped short of formally ordering Israel to halt its military campaign. Additionally, activists in the United States have filed a case against top officials in the Biden Administration, including the president himself, for complicity in genocide. However, in July 2024, a three-judge panel of the Ninth Circuit Court of Appeals upheld the dismissal of the lawsuit on the grounds that there is no judicial role in reviewing Executive Branch conduct related to foreign policy.

In 2007, Mahmoud Darweesh penned a poem titled "Silence

for Gaza," with lines that resonate as deeply today as they did then. Richard Falk refers to this poem in *Palestine: The Legitimacy of Hope*, noting its theme of resilience that speaks not only to Gaza but to all Palestinians, whether they live under occupation, in refugee camps, or in involuntary exile worldwide:

> *Enemies might triumph over Gaza (The storming sea might triumph over an island . . . they might chop down all its trees).*
>
> *They might break its bones.*
>
> *They might implant tanks in the insides of its children and women. They may throw it into the sea, sand, or blood.*
>
> *But it will not repeat the lies and say "Yes" to invaders.*
>
> *It will continue to explode.*
>
> *It is neither death, nor suicide. It is Gaza's way of declaring that it deserves to live.*

It is essential to note that the Palestinian people have not reacted to the conquest of their land with the same exclusivity demonstrated by the Israeli government. Instead, Palestinian leaders have called on the Jewish citizens of Israel to help build a truly democratic society for all. Yasser Arafat, in an interview with a US magazine, articulated that the land is meant for all who live on it, expressing a desire to coexist with full equality. This sentiment echoes in the words of Tawfiq Zayyad, the Palestinian poet and former mayor of Nazareth, who stated in solidarity with Native Americans that ". . . the future belongs to equality and brotherhood—And we oppressed people who struggle against injustice are the ones who will make this future a reality for all."

The poetry created by those who continued to reside in Palestine after 1948, as well as those outside the territories, has inspired many. This body of work is recited by schoolchildren across numerous countries, serving as a pivotal means of political and personal expression for a people whose rights have been systematically denied by the Israeli government. A resolution to this conflict cannot hinge upon statements from the Israeli right that demand Arabs simply surrender their rights to their homeland. Lasting peace cannot be built on an unjust foundation, it will come only when Palestinians regain their full rights to their ancestral land.

EDMUND GHAREEB
Washington, DC
March 2025

الفلسطينيون يمدون أيديهم
لصداقة الشعوب

IDENTITY CARD

Record!
I am an Arab
and my Identity Card
is number fifty thousand
I have eight children
and the ninth
     is coming in midsummer
Will you be angry?

Record!
I am an Arab
employed with fellow workers
     at a quarry
I have eight children
to get them bread
     garments
      and books
from the rocks—
I do not supplicate charity
     at your doors
Nor do I belittle myself
at the footsteps of your chamber
So will you be angry?

Record!
I am an Arab
without a name—without title
patient in a country
with people enraged
My roots—
     were entrenched before the birth of time
     and before the opening of the eras
     before the olive trees, the pines, and grass

My father—
        descends from the family of the plow
        not from a privileged class
And my grandfather—
        was a farmer
        neither well-bred, nor well-born
And my house—
        is like a watchman's hut
        made of branches and cane
This is my status
Does it satisfy you?
I have a name but no title.

Record!
I am an Arab
The color of hair—is black
The color of eyes—is brown
And my distinctive features:
        The head-dress is *hatta wi'gal*
        And the hand is solid like a rock
My favorite meal
is olive oil and *za'atar*
And my address:
        A village—isolated and deserted
        where the streets have no names
        and the men—work in the fields and quarries
        They like socialism
Will you be angry?

Record!
I am an Arab
You have stolen the orchards
of my ancestors
and the land
which I cultivated

Along with my children
And you left us with those rocks
So will the State take them
as it has been said?

Therefore!
Record on top of the first page:
I do not hate man
Nor do I encroach
But if I become hungry
The usurper's flesh will be my food
Beware—beware—of my hunger
and my anger!

TO MY BROTHER FATHI

For your sake, Fathi,
I broke the lock on my lips,
For you
I slaughtered silence in my heart
To write these lines
To build a wall in the face of death.
For you Fathi, believe me,
I cast the letters to make a sentence.

Fathi,
The sun that bathes the wounds of the fig trees
Its rays are dyed in blood by the executioners of Auares
That same sun toasts the wheat into gold in the fields
    of China
It wrings tears from the foreheads of peasants in our
    village.
You may not understand Fathi
But tomorrow you shall grow up
And the field will grow a green root before your eyes
And the lungs of the brown planter's sun will be
    crucified.
Who knows-
You may accept or reject the present reality;
If you reject you shall grow up,
If you acquiesce you become smaller.

Fathi
You may not understand
Why the East is tired of silence
Or why the dead vomited, and gave death
A bridge.
Or why your feet cried or why I wrote this

But tomorrow you shall grow and understand.
For your sake—for the children—
Believe me.

IN THE TWENTIETH CENTURY

For centuries
I did not hate
But now
I am forced to raise my untiring spear
In the face of the dragon,
To draw a sword of fire
In the face of Baal
To become Elijah in the twentieth century.

For centuries
I did not apostate
But now
I strike at the gods in my heart
The gods that sold my people
In the twentieth century.

For centuries
I did not turn visitors
Away from my door
Then one morning I opened my eyes
To find my food stolen
My wife strangled
And my child's back a field of wounds.
I recognized my treacherous guests.
I planted mines and daggers at my door
And I swore by the traces of the knife
That none of these guests shall enter my house
In the twentieth century.

For centuries
I was only a poet
In the bands of the *Sufis*

But now
I am an erupting volcano
In the twentieth century.

THE SKULL HARVEST

(This poem was written to commemorate the
Kafr Qassim massacre of 1966)

Did you hear the story of the skulls
how humans were slaughtered like cows
It is called the "Harvest of Skulls."
The stage is a village
Call it Kafr Qassim
It has awakened the town's people
At first they thought it was a dream
But the night went on and on
And the sleepy eyes opened again
This time they were shaken
by the wailing of bereaved mothers
and that of young men
of the elders, and the expectant
They exploded in our nation
volcanos of bitterness and revenge
A voice is coming from the horizon
The cries of victims crack their graves
Listen carefully:
A chant is shaking the village yard
It is the people, massacred by the guards

Unite your ranks and be prepared
to erase the misery
which lies heavily on your chest
to destroy a system based on oppression
to destroy a system of crime and blood

VICTIM NUMBER FORTY-EIGHT

They found a rosy lantern
and a moon
in his chest
while he lay dead
on a stone
they found a matchbox
and a travel permit
and tattoos on the arm
His mother kissed him
and mourned his death
month . . . after . . . month

When his brother grew up
and went to the market
to seek a job
he found himself
in a prison cell
he had no permit
he carried a box
with a bad smell
and another box

Oh children
of my country
that is how the moon died

JAIL AND CHILDREN

Don't be sad, Darling!
To put me in prison, as they did, is a very easy thing!
But what can they do about the sun
Shining outside and nurturing new rebels?

I should like to be romantic and say to you:
If my being in jail
Did nothing more than bring you to visit me
And cry in my arms—
Then my arrest was not in vain.

But I'm not feeling romantic right now!
*(How can one be romantic, with the bedbugs
                having such a feast?)*
I'm just scratching away, and writing to you,
And thinking about the dusk-colored guard,
And asking myself this banal question:
If I and others don't go to prison,
How will the prison guard
Feed his children?

Darling! I would so like for us
To have a baby!
We spoke of it once,
But I don't know if
We'll ever be given the chance.
That is why, for the time being, I give myself
To thoughts about the babies of others,
Including my enemies' babies!
And because they cannot understand this simple feeling
They put me here in prison.

TENT #50 (SONG OF A REFUGEE)

Tent #50, on the left, is my new world,
Shared with me by my memories:
Memories as verdant as the eyes of spring,
Memories like the eyes of a woman weeping,
And memories the color of milk and love!

Two doors has my tent, two doors like two wounds
One leads to the other tents, wrinkle-browed
Like clouds no longer able to weep;
And the second - a rent in the ceiling, leading
To the skies,
Revealing the stars
Like refugees scattered,
And like them, naked.

Also the moon is trudging there
Downcast and weary as the *UNRWA,*
Yellow as though it were the *UNRWA*
Under a load of yellow cheese for the refugees.

Tent #50, on the left, that is my present,
But it is too cramped to contain a future!
And - "Forget!" they say, but how can I?

> Teach the night to forget to bring
> Dreams showing me my village
> And teach the wind to forget to carry to me
> The aroma of apricots in my fields!
> And teach the sky, too, to forget to rain.

Only then, I may forget my country.

● مئـات الآلاف مـن
يهيمون عـلى وجوهه
الموت المحتم على أبدي

A REFUGEE

The sun crosses the frontier
the soldiers' bullets it does not fear
and the nightingale sings
at midday in Tulkarm
and eats supper in peace
with Jewish birds in the kibbutz
. . . a stray donkey feeds on the line
without a bullet in the spine
But I; a human, refugee
Oh land of my Homeland
my eyes and yours
are ever separate by a wall

AN ADDRESS

—1—

Hairs as short as my life is
And a mouth as sensuous as my dreams
And fire is her voice
And so is the music
Yet she wants me to rest
On an easy chair
And keep my thoughts clean.

Oh my dear hunter!
What you ask is much more
Than all that I can give . . .
For the angels are dead,
And I am not with them.

—2—

A wine was her perfume
Generous was her bed
But her hopes were stronger,
And the strongest of all:
She wanted my address.
She asked: "Where lives the 'Prince'?"
Then, I stood silenced
For I had no address.
I am a man in transit,
Twenty years in transit
A man who was even deprived
The right of having an address.

LOVER FROM PALESTINE

Your eyes
A thorn in my heart
Painful yet adorable
I shield it from the wind
And stab it deep through the night,
Through pain,
Its wound illuminates the darkness
Transforms my present into future
Dearer than my soul
And I shall forget as our eyes meet
That once we were together behind the gate.

Your words were my song
I tried singing
But winter replaced the spring
Your words, like the sparrow, flew away
Like the sparrow who left our doors
After you
Our mirrors broke—sorrows engulfed us
We picked the splinters of sound
And only learned to lament the fatherland.

We shall plant it together
Over the breast of a guitar
Play it over the roofs of our tragedy
To disfigured moons and rocks
But I have forgotten
I have forgotten your voice
Was it my silence
Was it my silence or
Your departure
That rusted my guitar?

I saw you last at the port
A lonely traveler without luggage
I ran to you like an orphan, a child,
Seeking answers in ancestral wisdom:
How could the green orchard be imprisoned,
Exiled, banished to a port
And still remain green

I entered in my diary:
I love oranges
And hate the port
Where I stood
As torrents of rain poured down
We only had the orange peels
And behind us stretched the endless desert.

I saw you on thorny hills
A sheepless shepherd—chased
I saw you on the ruins and once
You were a green orchard
I stood a stranger
Knocking at your door
The doors, the windows, the cemented stone
Vibrated.

I saw your face in the wells
In the granaries—torn
I saw you a waitress in the night cafés
I saw through the tears and wounds
And you are the words on my lips
You are the fire—
And the water.

I saw you at the mouth of a cave
Hanging your orphan's rags

I saw you in the stalls, in the streets
Warming your self by the fire
I saw you in the lamentations of misery
In blood dripping from the sun
In the salt of the sea and the sand
and yet
You were as beautiful as the earth
As children—

I swear
From my eyelashes I shall weave you
A kerchief
With words sweeter than honey
And kisses I shall write:
Palestinian you were
And so you will remain.

I opened my doors to the night storm
On a bronzy moon
I wandered the back streets in the darkness
And I have a date with words—
With the dawn of light
You are my virgin garden as
Faithful as the wheat
With our songs we shall pierce the air
And plant fertility in the dormant earth
And you like the braided palm tree
Unbending to the storm
Heedless of the hewer's blows
Beyond the claw and the fangs of the jungle beasts.

Come to me wherever you are
Whatever you have become
And return color to my cheeks
And meaning to my being

Return and take me into your eyes
Take an olive branch
Take a verse of my tragedy
A toy
Take a stone from our house
So that our descendants
Will remember their way home.

Palestinian are your eyes
Palestinian is your name
Palestinian your thoughts—dreams
Palestinian your mantilla, your body—
Your feet
Palestinian the words—the silence
Palestinian the voice
Palestinian in life
Palestinian in death.

I carried you in my diaries
Inspiration for the fire of my words
The food for my thoughts
And in your name I shout in the valleys:
Invaders' horses!— I met them
Though the times have changed
Beware—Beware hooves and stones
I destroyed the big idols
The thunderbolt has struck the flint
I shall fill the expanses of Sham
With my songs

In your name I have shouted to the enemy:
If I sleep
Let maggots eat my flesh
Ants cannot breed eagles
And the snake hatches only snakes.

Long ago
I turned away the invaders' horses
Deep in my soul
I know
I will turn them away again.

THE PSALM OF ISAIAH'S GRANDCHILDREN

We, Isaiah's grandchildren,
Call him.
We call to his kindly face
Trembling
Behind a veil of tears.
Isaiah's grandchildren
We call him—angrily crying:
O Isaiah you have slept for centuries.
In your absence the city became a harlot
Its silver tainted
Its wine diluted with water.
Tell them
O struggling Isaiah
Of the widows' bereavement.
Speak to them
Of this land's disgrace.

Alleluia.

The messengers of peace
Weep bitterly
For the innocent,
Their heads cut off
by the enemies of man.
Mournful Isaiah,
Arise today
And cry in this village
Tottering
On the brink of destruction,
Why do you prostitute yourself
Again, at the age of seventy,
With merchants from all the kingdoms?

Arise today.
Go up
And cry in the street of Tel Aviv:
Thousand woes to him
Who does not seek the Lord.
A thousand sorrows to him
Who goes into Egypt
Bringing the cross to the East.

Beloved Isaiah,
From the land of the Arabs
Comes a message:
Men of Tima;
Give water to the thirsty
Who seek refuge.

Bind the wounds of the fugitives
Fleeing before the sword
And
Give the hungry
A piece of bread.

Courageous Isaiah—arise!
And the children of Palestine
Will play again
Without fearing the serpent's bite,
And sheep may live in the wolves' den.

Alleluia.

The nations will adjudge
That no rights are lost
And voices are not silenced.
Struggling Isaiah!
The swords will be turned into plowshares

And the spears of the people into scythes.
No nation will raise its sword against another,
That little ones may not know war
Or bloodletting.
Alleluia—Alleluia.
God of Glory,
We warred too long.
We killed and were killed
Our blood was spilled
For centuries.
We spilled it.
God of glory, we have been tested too long
And we have come to rest.
Alleluia—Alleluia—Alleluia.

PSALMS OF THE PALESTINIANS

From here
From this purgatory
Of sorrow
In the Holy Land
The orphaned birds beseech
Mankind
From here
From Jeneen
From Old Jerusalem
Alleluia.

Once
A Gaza tune of yearning
Played
Once
The sad refrain
Kindled tragedy
In refugee tents
Once
In Jerusalem
The little ones chanted
We shall return
We shall return
Alleluia.

The birds nest on our roof
The sparrow flies
In the horizon

And in exile
Under the hot sun
In the wind

Hearts—eyes
Implored:
God of glory
Return us
Our trial
Has gone on too long!
Alleluia—Alleluia

And then it happened
The metallic eagles swept down
They did not bring the sons of Zion
To Zion
Not the remaining crowds
They did not bring
Pious psalms
To the wailing wall
God of glory!
What did they bring?
Do not ask me
For in my voice a pagan flame
Burns
And listen O God of glory
Listen to the outcry of a dispossessed people
We have been tested long enough
We have carried the weight of centuries
Long enough
        -Why aren't You convinced?-
Our days of trial have been too long
So
Return us—Return us
Alleluia—Alleluia—Alleluia.

THE GENERALS PSALM

Hear ye, O Israel, the voice of the prophets
And hear ye, O sons of Aaron, the call,
We send our command to all
To the wicked atheist
To the pious and devout.
Worship Washington's statues.
Stand up and worship them
Socialize with the idols of murderous Bonn
Sacrifice your sons at A.B.C.'s altar
In your hearts preserve it,
In its name raise populated homes,
On Canaan's feet
Kneel
O sons of Judah
Never mind if orchards
Become barren deserts
Alleluia—Alleluia.

JERUSALEM

I wept until my tears were dry
I prayed until the candles flickered
I knelt until the floor creaked
I asked about Muhammad and Christ
Oh Jerusalem, the fragrance of prophets
the shortest path between earth and sky
Oh Jerusalem, the citadel of laws
a beautiful child with fingers charred
and downcast eyes
You are the shady oasis passed by the Prophet
your streets are melancholy
your minarets are mourning
You, the young maiden dressed in black
who rings the bells in the Nativity
on Sunday morning?
who brings toys for the children on Christmas eve?
Oh Jerusalem, the city of sorrow
a big tear wandering in the eye
Who will halt the aggression
on you, the pearl of religions?
Who will wash your bloody walls?
Who will safeguard the Bible?
Who will rescue the Quran?
Who will save Christ?
Who will save man?
Oh Jerusalem my town
Oh Jerusalem my love
Tomorrow the lemon trees will blossom
and the olive trees will rejoice
Your eyes will dance
The migrant pigeons will return
to your sacred roofs

and your children will play again
and fathers and sons will meet
on your rosy hills
my town
the town of peace and olives.

A LETTER TO TWO CHILDREN ON THE EAST BANK

My vineyard, I wish I could fly
Fly
On the wings of yearning
But my longing . . . little one
Is chained,
Its wings broken.
Crossing to you has become impossible
Little one,
The river separates us
And they are stationed here
Stationed
Like a black curse.
They have demolished the bridges
And deprived me of you
Little one—and of passage.
(Death perches on the river.
Death awaits him who crosses.)

My vineyard, my gazelle
Pure honey that glimmers in the eyes
Estranges me.
And the blond braids, like wheat
Like the harvest season in our land
Estranges me awfully.
I wish I could fly, my gazelle,
Across the distance.
I wish I could fly.

As I sink into the sea
Of yearning And memory,
I run to the tape
And your voice fills the room:

Take me to Baisan,
To my winter village.
(O God—Baisan.
The land we had there,
The orange grove,
The wheat fields
Outstretched, as far as sight
Blessing my father with their gifts
Of wheat and fruits.
My father loved the land,
 He loved it.
"I will not sell if you
Give me its fill in gold"
He used to say.
But the Tartars raped the land
And your saddened grandfather died,
My little one.
He died grieving
There—in Baisan
Where his roots sank deep.)

The tape continues to play
Turning like time.
Now a childish story,
A chirping laughter then,
And Omar's joke.
Omar—
I ache from longing
To see your lovely face.
Do you remember the times you climbed the mountain
Bringing me bouquets of mountain flowers,
The gift of spring,
The gift of rain
In our land.

And I cross the river
On a bridge of imagination,
Of memory.
They would have killed that too
If they could.
They would have spilled the blood
Of love—of yearning—of remembrance.
And I embrace your childhood,
I kiss your forehead,
I kiss the eyes of love.
But
The surroundings return me to my humiliating reality.
Thorns and cactus pierce my ribs
And in my mouth the bitterness of certainty.

My beloved children
Across the river,
I have many stories to tell.
Not the stories of Sinbad,
Not the story of the Genii and the Hunter,
Of Aladdin and the princess,
But many new ones,
Stories that I fear to tell
Fearing they may
Put out the light in your world,
Frighten your childhood,
Rocking the anchors of safety and silence
In your island of innocence.
I fear for your little world,
I fear to tell you the
Horrible stories of the New Nazis
In our land,
That may turn your childish hair gray.

Do not ask when or how

It is going to end,
This tale of loss and separation.
You will not understand the answer today
And time will tell you when you grow up.

And then you will carry the weight
Like us,
Play your part
Like us.
Long is the book of our struggle,
Long is our story.
But you, my promised treasure,
You shall know
When and where the separated
Shall meet
And how the story of wandering and loss
Shall end.

MY LIBERTY

My liberty—my liberty—my liberty,
a sound I repeat
with angry lips
under the exchange of fire
and flames
I run after it
despite my chains
and follow its tracks
despite the night
and struggle ardently
for my liberty
My liberty
My liberty

And the Holy River
and Bridge repeat:
my liberty
and the two banks reiterate:
my liberty
and the raging wind and thunder,
tornadoes and rain
echo the sound:
my liberty

I shall carve its name
while I resist
on the land
by the walls
and the doors
in the Temple of the Virgin
in the altar
and the fields,

on every hill
and every valley
and every curve
and road
in prison
in the torture rooms
and on the gallows
Despite the chains
and the house demolition.
I shall carve its name
until I see it again
extending to my Homeland
and flourish
and flourish
until every inch of the land is covered
until every door is opened
by red liberty.
And the night vanishes
and the day breaks
My liberty—my liberty—my liberty

HAMZAH

1

Hamzah
was one of my townspeople
he struggled, like the rest
to earn his bread
with virtue and simplicity

He told me one day
while I strayed in defeat
Persevere, Oh cousin, Persevere!
Do not frail
this land is harvested
by the fire of crime
and shrunken in pain and silence
but her betrayed heart
is sparkling brisk

This land is a woman
the secret of fertility, they share
the ridges and the wombs
give birth to wheat and palms
and fighting men

The days have gone by
I did not see Hamzah, My cousin
but I did know
that the belly of the earth
is flowing like tide
in travail, for a child

2

That his father was sixty-five
has only fallen on deaf ears
And the governor issued his orders:
"demolish the house and punish the son
with torture"
He issued his order
and arose reciting slogans of love
security and order

The soldiers encircled the home
wriggled like the serpent
and the knocks commandingly heightened
enjoining the inhabitants to leave
Quite generously—in an hour or so

And Hamzah opened the windows
on looking at the soldiers and the sun
He exclaimed:
   "Oh Palestine, be assured
   the house, the children and myself
   will be sacrificed for your deliverance
   we live and die for your sake"

The echo of Hamzah's cry
sent a shiver through the nerves of town
and the house stood silent—and solemn

Not an hour yet
the house went up—and down
and the rubble of the rooms
housed the dreams
and the warmth which was
and the years of childhood

the memories of building
the struggle, and determination
tears and happy laughter

Yesterday
I saw Hamzah in the road
stepping forward
with firmness and faith
and upward brow

FROM BEHIND THE BARS
(NABLUS, OCCUPIED WEST BANK)

"A salute to our sons and daughters, the fighters that have been swallowed up by Israeli prisons."

1. The Will of Songs

Hell opened its doors
and swallowed the buds of the soft boy
in its dungeons
Yet the song remained there
on the lips of the young fighters
red and proud
penetrating the darkness and the walls:
— My brothers
      with my blood I write my will
      guard my revolution
      with your blood
      with my advancing nation
      I am *Fatah*, I am *Jabha*, I am *Asifa**

2. From "Hiba's" Diary

My mother's phantom hovers here
her forehead shines in my eyes
like the light of stars
She might be thinking of me now,
Dreaming

(Before my arrest
I drew letters on a book

---

* *Jabha* (the Front) and *Asifa* (the Storm) are liberation movements.

new and old
I painted roses
reared with blood
and my mother was near me
blessing my painting)

I see her
on her face silence and loneliness now
and in the house
silence and loneliness
My book case there on the book shelf
and my school's uniform
on the hanger
I see her hand extending
removing the dust from it
I follow my mother's steps
and listen to her thoughts
yearn to her hug and the face of day

3. From the Diary of " — "

*(There in Israel, our prisoners
whom we know nothing about.)*

From the ravine pours silent angry darkness
and night spreads its large sails here
the light of the stars and the dawn
cannot sneak in
A night without light
where our voices are lost
and the echo dies
and time cannot move

Time has lost its shoes here
it stood still

turning around the axis of stillness and boredom
confusing days and seasons
Is it the season for planting?
Is it the season for harvest?
Is it—who can say? No news
and the jailor stands, his face a stone
his eye a stone
robbing from us the sun, robbing the moon

4. To her Sister and Companion in Acts of Resistance

—I said it, as the beast wanted,
in the savagery of the investigation
forgive me Oh sister, beloved
I said "Yes" not because I could not bear
the harsh pain
not because one of the barbarians
kept hammering my bloody head to the wall
inventing torture, throwing me like a morsel
in the jaws of weakness
If this was all, I would have endured
with the patience of my stubborn pride
and the strength of faith and belief
But one beast among them wanted to—
Sister forgive me for I still
tremble
when I remember what I cannot say
But ten years of my life
will be chewed by bars
controlled by the jailor
I pay the atonement
for the moment of my surrender

5. From "Taiser's" diary[*]

Oh prison walls
what are
my brothers, beloved, and relatives
doing now?
Maybe the olive pickers are picking
Maybe the mountain olives
are moaning in the pressing-place
Maybe its blood is pouring
Oh bearer of the lamp
the oil is abundant
feed your lamp
and raise it for the travelers
for we promised to meet on the hill of Hitin
for we promised to meet on the mountains of Jerusalem

---

* Taiser is a student leader jailed in occupied West Bank.

ANTI-AIRCRAFT AMULETS

It is highnoon
The semi-circle of the sun beats down the street
The chickens cluck
As they hear the thump of heavy boots
And my father loads stupid bullets
Into the remnants of a rifle
Between the persistent calls of his
comrades:
The *Barwah* was lost
The battle rages at *Atleat.*

I was a child of nine
Then
I sucked the milk of tragedy
I was a child with dreamy eyes,
Thousands of nets surrounded me
On that day
I remember
Mother's troubled voice:
"Tonight
When you go to bed,
Sleep in your clothes
And don't take your shoes off!"
I did not understand what she meant then,
Yet—I cried.

It is nightfall
The semi-circle of the murdered moon,
cries in the street
And my father has not yet returned
The rumors speak of betrayals
By the high command

Of the soldiers' thrust—Backward
We cried.

The Army of Rescue
Run North like sheep
Throwing their guns
Into the trenches—
And their symbols of battle
Ooze downward—upon the mud
Army of Rescue
What a disgrace?

People of Ramah
The conqueror has arrived
Why sing songs of glory?
Aim all your amulets at the aircraft
Call for God's wrath
Throw the Commandments.
Al-Jifr
And all holy verses of heaven.

I was a child then—
they taught me that
The affairs of earth
Are in the hands of heaven
They taught me that He gives life
Or death
To whomever He chooses
They taught me to obey the prophets
Without asking,
Who are they?
And what have they done for the wretched?
They taught me to dance on a rope,
To humble women
To believe in witchcraft

To fear the nightfall!
They taught me what they wanted
Not what I needed
Saint George—will save me
They said
The words of theologians—will suffice

Defeated father—humbled mother
To Hell with
My inheritance of tribal teachings,
My savage rites
I cut the stupid customs
From the roots
I spit my hate
My shame
Into the faces of the devout
The holy ones
I kick the garbage of my defeat and
My humility
Into the face of the dervishes—
The barking half-men—the office holders

From the depths of my Hell
My voice prevails:
I condemn you to death
You,
The mud stuck on the sole of my
Great history,
And tailor a white cloak of death
From the skin of silent half-men
And if you wish to make
Etchings, crosses,
Stars, and crescents
Embroider them with your own hands.

TO THE POETS OF THE OCCUPIED TERRITORIES

Poets of the occupied land
your papers are immersed in tears and mud
your voices sound like the meanings of the hanged
your ink looks like the blood on butchered necks
We, the defeated poets
have been learning from you for years
We, the alien to history and to grief,
are learning how a letter resembles the knife

Poets of the occupied land,
You are the prettiest birds to fly out of captivity
Pure, like the prayers of the dawn
You are the roses growing from within the flame
You are the rain falling despite repression and defeat
You taught us how the drowned can sing
from the bottom of the sea
and how the grave can stand and walk
You taught us how to write poetry
for our poets have already died
they serve as butlers to the Prince
they brush his coat and pour him drinks
they are castrated
alas, it is the worst kind

Poets of the occupied land
You are a sunbeam shining through the door
You are a drumbeat marching out of the wilderness
Your names are carved on our eyelids
What can we tell you, friends?
about the literature of the "setback" and its poetry
We have, since June, been laying on pillows
entertaining ourselves with grammatical rules

suppressed—but not opposed to oppression
we mount wooden horses
and fight shadows and ghosts
and appeal loudly: Oh God of Gods
we are weak; and you are the victor and conqueror
we are poor; and you are the giver and provider
we are cowardly; and you are the forgiver

Oh poets of the occupied land
my nerves cannot endure
while the sanctity of Jerusalem is desecrated
and Saladin is among the looted
and the daughter of Dayan rambles around the altar
and we still call ourselves writers

Mahmoud Darweesh—greetings
Tawfiq Zayyad—greetings
Fadwa Touqan—greetings
You, who sharpen pencils on your ribs
we learn from you
how to explode mines in words
Poets of the occupied land
our "daraweesh" in the east
are still watching pigeons
drinking green cups of tea
If they stand beside your poetry
they would be dwarfed.

A GIRL AND A POEM

He promised to write me a poem
Since then, every morning I say:
Mother! *I'll go to the news-stand.*

My mother does not know that every morning
I steal a piece of my brothers' food
And with it buy a newspaper,
Hoping to find the promised poem there.

It is now two months that I buy papers with food
But the poem was never there.
Only today he phoned, and when I asked he answered:
That he wrote the poem long ago:
That the poem was written the moment he promised it
And that waiting for the poem, was the poem itself.

And now I feel empty!
Now I don't want to go to the news-stand.
Mother! *Why did he phone this morning,*
and stop the poem?

A POEM TO MAHMOUD DARWEESH

Without a sword—Without glories
Is this your Arabic voice—Coming to us from behind the
    wind—
To disperse us—to denude us
Is this the curse of the forefathers to the grandfathers?
Or is it the miscarriage of birth—
And the abortion of the twentieth clamour—
—The tumult of roses and festivities

And your wounded voice screams,
The tents burn while you are in the field
A sword—
        A sword—
        A flower—
Whose mention is hated by man—
And we hear your hurt voice while you are in the field
Men who spin the sun and the storms
Men who plant corruption
Then you come
And you express, in spite of this restriction, willingly you
    come
So we drink the perfume of our valley
And we glance at your sad face from beneath the wind
    and rain
And we see in it—our expatriation
Our deserts, the hardships of travel
Your forehead: a tent
Your palms: two broken ploughs
And your wound is a real flower from Beisaan
That flaps and flaps in dreams
"Palestinian by fringes and name
The tattoo is Palestinian—

Palestinian by clemency—"
And you are a pigeon that fell on the wires
And you are the eagle in the sky
But yes—we were stabbed in the forehead when the
    sight was blurred
Twice were we crucified and nothing did we
    accomplish—
But we are, like your voice, still alive
And inspite of their bullets we still survive—

ON POETRY

1

Yesterday,
We sang to a star above a cloud
To a full moon near the star
And cried.

Yesterday
We reproved the vines,
The moon, the night, the fate
And flirted with women.

The clock has struck, and Khayyam drinks
While we remain wretched,
Listening to his opiating songs.
My poet friends
We live in a new age,
The past is dead
And he who writes poetry
In the age of the storms, of the atom
Is a prophet.

2

Our poems are
Colorless, aimless, voiceless
If they do not carry the lamp
From house to house.
And if simple do not comprehend
Throw your poems to the wind
And let us immortalize silence.

3

If only these poems were
A chisel in the hands of a worker
A grenade in the hands of a fighter
If only
If only these poems were
A plow in the hands of a peasant
A shirt, a door, a key,
If only
                    once
A poet said:
If my poems gratify my friends
And anger my enemies
Then I am a poet.

And I shall say—

REFLECTIONS IN THE STREET

Street of lights
What color is the sky?
And why
Why do they dance?
How do I go by
Past breasts on breasts
And thighs embracing thighs?
What use is it to cry?
Tears have never stopped
The hurricane
Save your tears
And march on.

My fate is sealed
In the arrogance of time
I walk colorlessly
Between wakefulness and sleep
Searching for words,
Climbing walls
Cursing in the mud
The sun rises
Then darkness falls
And the dove remains a symbol of peace.

Street of lights
What color is the darkness?
And why?
Why do they dance?
When will my friend of yesterday
My tormentor
Stop her singing—her betrayals?
Is it the sound of jazz beckoning her?

But I too call her
The sound of jazz is artificial
My voice speaks of the
Melting heart
Under the wheel of night.

Once, I could dry
O calmness of the prophets!
But the flame refuses to meet winter.

From what grave do you come,
My grandfather's face,
The unsmiling face of a prophet?
And your suit the color of blood on dried stone
And your overcoat the color of mud
Grandfather,
Unsmiling prophet,
From what grave do you come,
To make me a poisoned statue?
My debt is great
But I did not yield an inch,
I did not submit
Yet
They danced and sang over your grave.
But go back to rest
For I am awake
Awake until the end.

REFLECTIONS ON THE TRAGEDY—I MOURN (1967)

My friends, I mourn for the language of the past and
    the old books
The discourse, punctured, like battered shoes,
The verse of profanity, slander, aspersion
I mourn—I mourn—
The thought which finally brought defeat.

II

Bitter to our mouth is poetry
Bitter to our eyes is beauty
The night—the curtains—the seats
Bitter is the cup of life.

III

Oh my sad Homeland
You have changed me overnight
From a poet of love and longing
To one who writes with a knife.

IV

Our feeling now transcends that love
We are ashamed—we must write with a knife

V

No wonder we lost the war
We entered it
With the oratorical art of the Orient
And the innocuous sonnets of Antar
We entered with the logic of the drum and the lute.

VI

The secret of our tragedy
Our clamor rings louder than our voice
Our swords stand higher than our bodies.

VII

The summation of our case is reduced to a sentence
We adopted the facade of civilization
While our spirit remained antiquated

VIII

The flute and the lute
Do not secure victory.

IX

Our extemporaneous ways
Brought us fifty thousand new tents.

X

Do not curse the sky for having foresaken you
Do not blame the circumstances
God grants victory to whomsoever he wishes
No one of you can produce swords.

XI

It aches me to hear the news in the morning
And to hear the dogs bark.

XII

The Zionists did not cross our frontier
They infiltrated our gaps like ants.

XIII

Five thousand years we spent surreptitiously underground
Penniless—beards unshaven and eyes like *ports* for the
    flies
My friends, try to demolish the doors
Try to purify your thought—cleanse the garments
My friends, try to read a book . . . write a book
Plant letters like grapes and plums
Try to sail to the land of snow and fog
You are unknown in your hiding underground
You are taken for a species of wolves.

XIV

Our skin is senseless
Our soul suffers from bankruptcy
Our days revolve around chess, drowsiness, visitation
Are we truly the best nation?

XV

We run in the streets
With ropes under arms
We climb without knowledge
We break the glass and the locks
We curse like frogs—we praise like frogs
Our heroes suddenly become dwarfs
Our nobles suddenly become dastardly
We improvise courage
While sitting in the Mosque
Idiotic—and lazy
Composing verse—and reciting proverbs
Supplicating victory over the enemy
From Divine Providence

XVI

Our oil which floods the desert
Could have become a burning spear
But to the dismay of the noble in *Qureish**
And the disgrace of *Nizar* and *Awse***
We spilled it at the maiden's feet.

XVII

If I am granted amnesty
If I can meet with the Sultan
I would say: My master Sultan
Your fierce dogs have torn my suit
I am constantly haunted by your spies
Their eyes—noses—feet are behind me
Determined as destiny
They interrogate my wife
And compile a list of my friends . . .
Your Majesty, because I approached your discreet walls
To express my grief and calamity
I was struck by the shoe and then forced to bite it by
     your soldiers
My master—my Sultan, you were defeated twice
Because half of our people are speechless, suppressed
Can people live without a tongue?
Surrounded by ants
Confined within walls—
If I am granted amnesty against the soldiers
I would say to the Sultan
You lost twice because you were unenlightened about
     human rights.

---

* *Qureish* is the tribe from which the prophet Muhammad came.
** *Nizar* and *Awse* are famous Arab tribes.

XVIII

If we had not laid unity to rest in the sand
If we had not sliced her tender body with the spear
If we had kept it secure in our hearts
The dogs would not have eaten our flesh.

XIX

We want an angry generation
To aim towards the horizon
To search the roots of history
And penetrate the annals of thought
We want a generation with new features
Unforgiving—unwilling to overlook mistakes
Unbending—unaccustomed to duplicity
We want a lofty generation—with imposing height.

XX

Oh children,
From the Ocean to the Gulf, you are the blossom of hope
The generation which shall destroy the chains,
Extinguish the opium in our heads
And rid us of our sluggishness.
Oh children,
You are still innocently uncorruptible
Cleanhanded . . . as the dew and snow
Do not read the history of our generation
We are vanquished
Insipid like the watermelon rind
Punctured like old shoes.
Do not study our news
Do not track our footsteps
Do not accept our thought
We are the generation of sickness and consumption

Deceit and acrobatics.[*]
Oh children,
You are the spring rain, the blossom of hope
The seed of fertility in our somber life
You are the generation which shall conquer defeat.

---

[*] He means unsteady and can be easily swayed.

AL-FATH

—And after we were killed
and after we received the prayer of the dead
and were laid to rest
and after our bones decayed
and our skeletons crumbled
and after we became hungry—and thirsty
and after we repented
but then disbelieved in the Almighty
and after we despaired
after — and after
FATH has emerged
as a beautiful rose comes out of a wound
as a cold spring water in arid land
and suddenly,
the coffins rebelled
and, like Christ, we rose from the dead

They appear, however late they may be
they appear in the grain of wheat
on the Lemon tree
and on the branches and the wind
in our conversation and the sound
and in our mother's tears
and our martyr's eyes
They appear, however late they may be
on the path to Ramallah
and the Mount of Olives
They inhabit the dark of night—the caves—and things
they grow out of sorrow, mighty trees
and they create out of the rocks, bundles of flowers
they have no papers of identity

and no names
but they still appear

Oh *FATH*, you are the Shore
we glanced after having gone astray
you are the sun of midnight
which rose after much delay
you are the breeze of Spring
which moistened our barren land
when we looked forward to fifty centuries
and rose very high
Our lives blossomed
after having withered away
Oh *FATH*, you are a beautiful horse
whose forehead reflects Beisan and Jalil
and Gaza, Jerusalem, the birds, and the Plain
You're our water—our snow—and shady tree
You're the infant whose face we longingly awaited
Oh *FATH*, we are Mecca awaiting the Prophet

Oh *FATH*, a year has gone away
and the dagger of Israel remains in our back
we search our graves in the dark
idiotically, as we did yesterday
echoing the fairy tale:
"Patience is the Key to salvation"
and we still think that God in heaven
will restore for us our position
and we still think that Victory
is a feast to be offered while we sleep
and we still sit, as for years past,
on the sidewalks of the United Nations
to beseech (beg) the agencies to grant
        milk and flour

misery, sardines, and second-hand trousers
and we still rustically echo our favorite wisdom:
"Patience is the Key to salvation"
the bullet, not patience is the Key

Oh God,—we refuse, after today, to be pure
for the pure and virtuous—are half-dead
They stole our homeland
and killed our children
permit us, oh God, to be killers.
We refuse, after today, to be innocent
        like a lamb
we refuse to remain dizzy and capricious
oh poetry, be angry
oh prose, be bitter
oh mind, be rebellious
lest we all become a flock of refugees.

ENEMY OF THE SUN

I may - if you wish - lose my livelihood
I may sell my shirt and bed.
I may work as a stone cutter,
A street sweeper, a porter.
I may clean your stores
Or rummage your garbage for food.
I may lie down hungry,
O enemy of the sun,
But
I shall not compromise
And to the last pulse in my veins
I shall resist.

You may take the last strip of my land,
Feed my youth to prison cells.
You may plunder my heritage.
You may burn my books, my poems
Or feed my flesh to the dogs.
You may spread a web of terror
On the roofs of my village,
O enemy of the sun,
But
I shall not compromise
And to the last pulse in my veins
I shall resist.

You may put out the light in my eyes.
You may deprive me of my mother's kisses.
You may curse my father, my people.
You may distort my history,
You may deprive my children of a smile
And of life's necessities.

You may fool my friends with a borrowed face.
You may build walls of hatred around me.
You may glue my eyes to humiliations,
O enemy of the sun,
But

I shall not compromise
And to the last pulse in my veins
I shall resist.
O enemy of the sun
The decorations are raised at the port.
The ejaculations fill the air,
A glow in the hearts,
And in the horizon
A sail is seen
Challenging the wind
And the depths.
It is Ulysses
Returning home
From the sea of loss

It is the return of the sun,
Of my exiled ones
And for her sake, and his
I swear
I shall not compromise
And to the last pulse in my veins
I shall resist,
Resist—and resist.

WE SHALL REMAIN

It is a thousand times easier
For you
To pass an elephant through the needle's eye
To catch fried fish in the milky way
To plow the sea
To teach the alligator speech,
A thousand times easier
Than smothering with your oppression
The spark of an idea
Or forcing us to deviate
A single step
From our chosen march.
Like twenty impossibles
We shall remain in Lydda, Ramlah, and Galilee.

Here upon your chests
We shall remain
Like the glass and the cactus
In your throats
A fiery whirlwind
In your eyes

Here, we shall remain
A wall on your chests.
We wash dishes in the hotels
And serve drinks to the masters.
We mop the floors in the dark kitchens
To extract a piece of bread
From your blue teeth
For the little ones.

Here, we shall remain
A wall on your chests.
We starve,
Go naked,
Sing songs
And fill the streets
With demonstrations
And the jails with pride.
We breed rebellions
One after another.
Like twenty impossibles we remain
In Lydda, Ramlah, and Galilee.

Here, we shall remain.
You may drink the sea;
We shall guard the shade
Of the olive tree and the fig,
Planting ideas
Like the yeast in the dough.
The coldness of ice is in our nerves
And a burning hell in our hearts.
We squeeze the rock
To quench our thirst
And if we starve
We eat the dirt
And never depart
Or grudge our blood.

Here—we have a past
            a present
                and a future.
Our roots are entrenched
Deep in the earth.
Like twenty impossibles

We shall remain.
Let the oppressor review his account
Before the turn of the wheel.
For every action there is a reaction:
Read what is written in the Book.
Like twenty impossibles
We shall remain—in Lydda, in Ramlah
and Galilee.

THE FALL OF THE MASKS

All the masks have fallen
either my flag remains
and my cup
or my corpse
and a hurricane

All the masks have fallen
and the diamond cover
on your eyes
Oh man without manhood:
the executioner of my dream.
The marble statutes have fallen
and your tears.
Oh alligator of time,
All have fallen
and the Hawks nest
for twenty years:
"I am the pigeon's nest
Oh conscience of the earth"
Your sad songs have fallen,
and your miserable epics.
You who dreamt of an obedient earth
and registered it on your accord
to suit your commonplace desire
all the masks have fallen
shattered around four winds
In what God will you seek shelter?
Which God will bless your napalm?
and the fragments which tore my flesh?
Who will sell you a writ of absolution?
While your teeth are deep in my arm
You who fear the glow

and begrudge fertility
in the land of the hungry
You, the stooge of colonialism
the agent of skyscrapers
and guardian of petroleum
which flows in the midst of wolves

My blood vessels were made into pipe
for the oil of invaders who came from the fog
My blood vessels were made into snakes
and ropes to chain the oppressed
my wounded people
I dug my way from the well to the light
You who fear the light
and I demolished the dark walls with my teeth
and exclaimed to the torn generation
of the desert:

Forward in the name of life—forward
and your sword appears in the dark
while I tighten my belt
and raise my forehead
despite repression
and you still shout:
"Oh conscience of the world
who will safeguard the *diaspora*
from the Arab mob?"
And you press your teeth harder in my arm
while I build a High Dam
and dream of schools
factories and pasture
You who fear schools, factories and pasture
and the wheat immersed with tears and blood
of those who work from dawn to dusk
and the starved revolutionaries

All the masks have fallen
either my flag remains
and my cup
or my corpse
and a hurricane
Oh esteemed Security Council
My story has twenty chapters

Oh esteemed Security Council
It became twenty nights
twenty orange flowers
decayed in the square
of our humble village
twenty orange flowers
roaming at night
in the streets of the city
twenty sad caravans
departing ashamedly
with heads below
to the east- I remember
to the south and north
searching for a God
twenty orange trees
were butchered there
without fight

And I suffer
from my torment
while my worn feet
go from door to door
and my swollen face
unaware of spears
and my children's face
like an empty plate

Esteemed Security Council
for twenty years
I called on you
and today, through the storms
which threaten peace
my voice reaches you
by air mail
from the forest of blood
fire, bitterness and tents
It comes to you as a red rose
in the new year:
Whoever comes to my home to kill
will be taken away in a box

Oh ancient Security Council
my voice comes to you as a red rose
from the field of crime
farewell—farewell—
until we meet again
ancient Security Council
in the old city
of Jerusalem

JOB'S DIARY

For Export

I have plenty of God's favors
I have curses—orphanhood—sorrow
I have hunger—debt—exile
Of all shades and colors
I have them—retail for export
I have plenty of God's favors
Many rules—official records
Stacks of laws that never crossed a mind
I have wonders for all times
At retail for export
Profit is guaranteed by God
And good intentions

My heart is like a star
At times
A ball of copper
At times
A hand grenade
My heart—at retail for export
Profit is guaranteed by God
And good intentions
I have plenty of God's favors
At retail for export.

JOB'S DIARY

I Shall Tell the World

I shall tell the world—tell them
Of the lamp they shattered in my home,
Of the axe that destroyed a lily
Of the fire that consumed a braid

I shall tell them of the unmilked ewe-lamb
Of the morning coffee—left undrunk
Of the mother's dough left unbaked
Of the mud roof where the grass grows now
I shall tell the world.

Neglected daughter of my neighbor
I still have your doll—put away
I have it so come back
Come back
On the train of the East wind.

And Hanna
I have forgotten your features
Yet, I ache to remember
In my heart I hear your footsteps
How beautiful we were—together
My neighbor's daughter, Hanna and I.

How beautiful together we were
So why have our eyes
Become focused in foreign land?
And our hands roped
To this curse?
I shall tell the world—tell them
I shall tell the world!

JOB'S DIARY

5/5/67

—The morning music . . . silly!

—The coffee is scarce, my guest
Let us drink our coffee light, today.

Smoke . . .

"Our first news release:
Levi Eshkol declared:
    The slithy toves did gyre and gimble
King Hussein says:
    The Jabberwock came whiffling and burbled.
America has lost one of her ships.
McNamara threatened."

—Son of . . .
—Moron!

—Today I report this story:
    Ernesto Che Guevara
    Builds a moon
    In some horizon.

JOB'S DIARY

As Usual

As usual
It is provocative today.
The toll of dead rises in Haiphong,
In Aden they killed six children.
In Israel—mourning.
They commemorate the victory
Over Nazism,
The memory of human slaughter.
The Army chief of staff
                threatens Syria!

7/5/67

Nothing new.

JOB'S DIARY

12/5/67

All the reports declare:
I never fought against God
Why am I taught by pain—?
Well!

Hear me
Whisper into the image:
Job's curse arise
Arise
Job's curse . . . revolt
And listen to my cry:
Job
Do not submit to agony
    resist the pain!

Note:

To the readers
The remaining notes of Job's diary are drowned in "red
ink"—It is impossible to read—please excuse.

I, THE PRONOUN OF THE SPEAKER

I am the hunger of him who has worked since dawn,
I am the song of return,
I am the road into the fields,
I am thousands of brown palms
Coming to rest on door handles.
I am the promises, the shouts of joy,
The tears embroidered on the handkerchief of exile.

I am the mint on the hills.
I am the spring, the rose cane.
I am the deserted fire place
And the roof—
I am the ear of wheat.
I am the trees, the robin.
I am the tanned shepherd, the flute.
I am the wet breeze in the sea,
The sails, the night trip, the shore.
I am waiting for the absent child.
I am the strip of land, the plow.
I am the strength of the peasant
Working in the earth.
And, out of my flesh a garden grows
And children, and bread, and books!

I was the professor of mathematics,
The blind singer, the guitar.
I was the woodcutter, the hunter, and
Among other things, the shouts, the forest, the groom.
I was the yards, the vineyards, the fortune teller.
I was the student of night, of the stars,
Under my cover lived the voice of the tribes,
Under my blanket lived the planters' village,

The glistening of the grass,
The clanging of the picks and the grain harvesters.
On my ancient face
Passed thousands of caravans
Carrying coffee and spices.
My ribs produced a bridge,
(before they became a refinery for *Aramco Oil)*
Upon it passed the yellowed books
To Athens, Misapur, and old India,
In their travel on the road, undisturbed
By the ghosts of obscured centuries,
And my ideas lighted darkened Europe.
So why do they cover the bridge with napalm?
With my tears, with my guys, with my hate?
Why do they drive away the sun
On the night of crime
In the Forties my face was bloodied
Oh, world, my lungs have become like
A sad blacksmith's bellows.
My words have turned into an ember,
A whip, a commando.
Do you hear oh world?
Even the tulips became horns
Signaling
My burning in refugee tents
And I grew them for century upon a century.

One year falls upon another
            and my face falls in the dust
One year falls upon another
            and my dialogue continues.
My words are strong like an unbroken mare.
My voice is like an unpolished bell
In the imprisoned halls,
The halls of delegations, of neckties,

Of whiskey
And I do not meet refined gentlemen
Who carry this earthly planet in their briefcases
From the gates of one airport to another.
My words are like an unbroken mare.
My voice is like an unpolished bell.
And
This is why they made carpets of my skin
Drapes, and mops at the seat of the UN.

This is why the hawks claw my children
And this is why I am marked
On all lists for execution.

Well—
For the twentieth time: Thanks.
Someday at the seat of the UN
The world will commemorate my eagles,
My massacre, with a crown of thorns.
Someday, with my hands
I will transform the image.

A DIALOGUE WITH A MAN WHO HATES ME!

Rome was burnt, O crazy man
Rome is more durable than Nero
Rome will not grasp your poems
She can recite them by heart
Rome will slice your strings
My tunes arise from my heart
Your voice echoes a miserable past
My voice echoes a rocket rage
Your path is long
I shall not tire
Yehuda sold you
I shall not be crucified
My ancestors were cremated in Auschwitz
My heart is with them
Pull out the wires from my skin
And the wounds of yesterday?
A shameful scar—in the face of the executioner over there
What do you carry in your head
A little wheat
What's in your chest?
A *picture of a wound*
Your face reflects a rancor color
My face reflects the color of earth
Then convert your sword into plowshare
You did not leave me land to plow
You criminal!
I did not steal—did not kill—didn't oppress
You Arab! You are a dog!
O man, may God cure your soul
Why don't you try the taste of love
Why don't you make way for the sun!!

ABOUT A MAN

They chained his mouth
And tied him to the rock of death
And decreed: You're an assassin
They hid his clothes and banners
They took away his food
They plunged him into the death chamber
And proclaimed: You're a marauder.

They ejected him from every port
They took his beloved little girl
And declared: You are a refugee.

Tell your excited eyes and ensanguined hands:
Night will be gone
The prison and chains will not remain
Nero had died, but Rome was alive
She fought on with her eyes.
The seeds of a withering ear of wheat
Will fill the plain.

A SONG FOR MEN

I walked towards the river
Do not fear for my feet
from the thorns.
My footsteps are like the sun
they can't be tenacious without blood

I walked towards the river
Do not fear for my heart
from the pirates.
My heart is blended with earth;
It is a breeze in the hands of love,
and gunpowder in the face of hate

I walked towards the river
Do not worry about my eyes
from the desert
The bitterness of grief
shall be sweetened
by my green forest
and transmuted into wine

I walked towards the river
even with battered shoes
and eyes opened
without stop
or desire to sleep
for those who sleep
will lie in a bed,
a wooden box

Upward, our throats
Upward, our quarries

Upward, our hopes
Upward, our songs

We shall make ladders
for tomorrow
from our gallows
and our cross
And we shall exclaim:
Oh *Radwan,* open the door.

We shall fire poetry
from our throats
and transcend our wailing
make it into wine
to be served in the festival
and sung in the streets
in the factories
in the quarries
in the fields
and in the clubs

We shall change the quarry
into an observation post
overlooking the deepest
and the farthest scenes
We shall only view the dawn
and hear of triumph.
Every insurrection will move us
And every maiden will kiss us
And every garden will feed us
We shall dance to every verse
and assist every orphan

We shall leave the camp
and our exile

We shall leave the hiding place
and be cursed by the enemy:
"Hey Arabs—uncultured."
Yes. Arabs—and unashamed.
We know how to handle the sickle
and how the armless resists
and how to build a modern factory
a home
        a hospital
            a school
                a bomb
                a missile
and how to compose music
and write beautiful verse
sentimental, rhythmic, intellectual

        Voices:

And what then?
We already heard
your phosphoric voice
We heard—we heard—
Could words make a palace
out of a hut?
Your path is curvy
and your people—
are shedding tears
for their glorious past
and your land—
is like a carpet
at crossroads.
And you—a destitute
What then—what then?
Your voice, over the north wind
is beautiful—but we are bored

Answer

You are lowly, like tar
You are meek
hiding behind curtains of boredom
You are gullible—like the moon
crucified on a rock.
Let me finish my song
carry the northern wind
and suppress the hurricane
in my sleeves
Let me store dynamite
in my blood
You are lowly, like tar
and gullible—like the moon

Song of the Troy Women

Farewell, nights of chastity
Farewell, walls of Troy
We left our hiding
to attend the weddings
of the invaders
to dance over the bodies
of our men
We are the spoils
they took away our virginity
and all they desired
They are degenerate and vicious
We lay in their chambers
the killers of our heroes
Farewell, nights of chastity
and dreams
We are the spoils

since today
And the relics of Troy
    Comments on the Song

Yes, I heard the tune
Do not surrender
your flute to death
It shall blossom light and verse
and melt the steel
pave the road
and guard our bodies
against opium injection
Let's burn the feathers
of the past
and play a beautiful tune
My will—and yours
My flesh—and yours
will pave the street
of the future

    Voice

What then—what then?
Your people shed tears
for their glorious past
and the tunes of captivity
will dig for those
who resist the grave

    Answer

You are lowly, like tar
and gullible like the moon
Look back a little

Oh sad voice
You ride a camel
While others mount a rocket
Look back a little
Look back to history

With Christ

Hello, is Christ there?
Yes, who are you?
I am calling from Israel
My feet are nailed
And a thorny wreath
is in my hands
Which way should I go
Oh Son of God
Which way?

Should I submit and be exempted
or resist and face torment
I say to you, proceed
forward, oh people.

With Muhammad

Hello, is Muhammad of Arabia there?
Yes, who are you?
A prisoner in my land
without a homeland
without education
without a home.
They expelled my folks
and silenced my voice
as the price of *freedom*
What should I do?

Confront the jail
and challenge the warden
for the sweetness of faith
will wipe out bitterness

With Hapcock

Hello—Hello
Is Hapcock there?
Yes, who are you?
I am an Arab sir
I used to have arms
to cultivate the land
which my father fertilized
I used to have a robe
a turban and drums
I used to have—
Enough, my son
Your story is close to my heart

The Rest of the Song

Let me finish my song
The gift of the forefathers is:
"We planted—so you may reap the harvest."
Their voice is like fertilizer
It floods the desert with rain
and makes the barren trees bloom.

Let me
With the Congo—with the jungle
with the bodies
whose noble tears
intoxicate the forest

Let me finish my song
With the Danube—the Jordan
and the Volga
With the rivers, the falls
and the flowers
And where the trees
embrace the nightingale
I am one of them,
a flute in the orchestra
of those who wiped off the dust
of yesterday,
and embraced the sun
and the glorious future.
I am stronger and taller
than the dark cell
Yes, I am an Arab
I repeat—and unashamed.

I DECLARE

As long as a hand-span of my land remains
As long as I have an olive tree—
A lemon tree—
A well—and a cactus plant
As long as I have but a single memory
A tiny library
A grandfather's picture—and a wall
As long as Arabic words are uttered
And folk songs are sung
In my land
Scribes of poetry
Tales of *Antar Al-Abse*
Epics of the wars against Persia and Rome
As long as I possess my eyes
Lips and hands
My own-self!
I shall declare in the face of my foe!—
A fierce struggle of liberation
In the name of free men everywhere
Workers—students—and poets—
I shall declare—
And let the cowards—*enemies of the sun*
Be satiated of the bread of shame
As long as I have myself
As long as myself remain
My words will remain—
Bread and arms—
In the hands of freedom fighters!

LETTER FROM EXILE

A kiss for you and—salutations
What else should I say
Where to begin and where to end
Time flows away without restriction
And all I have in exile stored:
A loaf of bread, moldy and hard
A copybook full of disappointments
And longing for my beloved
Where shall I begin

All that was said
Or will be said
Could not return me home
Nor will it bring rain
Or grow feathers on an aging bird

A message in *Listener's Mail.*
Tell her I am well
I tell the sparrow:
"Do not forget, If you're ever there
Tell her I am well"

Well o well
I still can see
The sky is not moonless
My clothes are not yet torn
Although there are patches—here and there
But it's all right now

I am now grown- over twenty
The burdens of life I shoulder like men
I work in a tavern, as dishwasher
And coffee maker

You should see me Ma
A smile on my face
For the customer's sake!

I also smoke and stand at the corner
To speak with the girls
Like other young men
Life is unbearable without women.

I am well
I have a loaf of bread
And some vegetables

I heard on the radio
Messages of the exiles
They all concurred, without dissent:
"We are quite well."
No one has said: "I am distressed"
Or "It's wretched here."

How's my father?
Does he still pray?
Does he love children, the land and olives
As he always did?
And how are my brothers
Did they graduate?
Are they teachers now?
Like my father used to say

Do you know what grieves me sometimes
Suppose I fell ill
Will the night pity me
Will the tree under which I fell
Recognize my body as that of a man
And give it protection from hungry beasts

My dear Mother
Why did I write these letters
There is no mail
The land, sea, and air are blocked
And you all might be dead
Or perhaps alive without address

Should we go on
No country—no home—no flag—no address

DEFIANCE

You may fasten my chains
Deprive me of my books and tobacco
You may fill my mouth with earth
Poetry will feed my heart, like blood
It is salt to the bread
And liquid to the eye
I will write it with nails, eye sockets and daggers
I will recite it in my prison cell—
In the bathroom—
    In the stable—
        Under the whip—
            Under the chains— .
                In spite of my handcuffs
I have a million nightingales
On the branches of my heart
Singing the song of liberation.

TAXATION

Taxes of every type and stamp
Leave us indigent and penniless
Our children craving
Wandering amidst the dump
To pick some remnants of food
Abandoned by affluent breed
While their brats are boneless
Like balls of fat
They do not speak
Nor do they smile
But—always they eat
Like chickens, they grow in a cage
But theirs are made of glass
Cages of ore and ivory.

Our women are miserable and shabby
They are the wretched of the earth
The bodies are old—but they are young
The stories are sad and news is bad
Their women are dressed in velvet
They sleep on fleecy beds
They drink and play in the middle of the night

From where does this abundance come
While the skies are reluctant to give
Not even a little drop
In spite of prayers morning and night
But if they consent to give us gold
The *Master* will be eager to seize
And we would pack it in his mouth
And in his eyes—ears and nose.

From where does the money come
It had become a mere hope
And dreams of an oppressed class
Whose chains are heavy on the necks
He lay idle, unemployed
But always diligent in his search
And when he has lost all hopes of work

He sold the house which he erected
And sold the lantern and the wick
To feed his craving little ones
To preserve their life and some of their youth
But the tax collector thrust himself
A greedy face and an abject past
His motorcade includes the police
The hungry masses rise to their feet
Their blood is boiling in the veins
And their throats explode like thunder sound
But where—does the money come from
Nothing remained except the young
Who are on sale in the market place.

But—
Oh thieves, I have a question to raise:
What do you do with the money we pay?
And who profits from our funds?
Where does it go, oh ruling clique
Where does it go, we aren't unaware
We have been taught through years past
You wish to convert our land into graves
And dance on the ruins of our estate
But you will not fulfill your aims
For the grip of the poor will crush your might
And quell the force of the war lords
A solid peace will prevail and reign

We'll live for the young and throw the chains
The hearts of mothers will unstrain
And our glees will echo upon the horizon.

TRUTH IS SAID

I say that I hate occupation
you get angry
wake the mountain from its sleep
and chide the fox for forgetting
and you draw the arrest order

I say that I hate war and fighting
you get angry
send an armed messenger
polite
to tell me: Come!
and when I smile
you drown in insults and coughs

I say that I hate oppression
and that all I have
of progressive papers is *Al-Ittihad*
you get angry
and from the sky
you pour *Jerusalem* and *The News*
al-Subh and *al-Masa*
and *New Outlook*
and other names

I say that I hate rape
you get angry
and honor me in a prison cell
and inflict punishment upon me
and guard me from my friends
I say that I love Justice
you hate it!

I say that I hate injustice
you love it
and if you get angry
there is the ocean
drink it!

.

I DEFY

Talk about exile—I defy
silence my argument with
chains and a foolish prison cell
I defy

Turn plague and sadness against me
I remained defying
cut my wrist
with my bloody chest I defy
cut my leg
I mount the wound and walk
and with my violence I defy
with my forehead I defy
and with my teeth
and the teeth of songs—I defy

and kill me—I defy
I kill death
and come to you a defying God

All what I own of my father's and grandfather's
inheritance is to defy!

All what I understand from the wind
and the secrets of erased villages
and the songs of springs
on dying grass
a concealed sob
the roots of the tree
memorize it for me
a sob: To defy

All the eyes of children living within me
in bloody exile
All what I live of my absent country
in name and deed
a scream bruising me—to defy!

My anger drips oil and honey
my pain bears almonds, flouts and roses
so jail my piece of bread
I defy

THE CHILDREN OF RAFAH

To him who digs his path
in the wounds of millions
whose tanks crush the garden's roses
To him who breaks at night the houses' windows
who burns a field and a museum
and sings to the fire
who rips the hair of sad women
and bombs grape fields
who executes the nightingale of feasts in the square
whose planes bombard children's dreams
who breaks rainbows
The children of deep rooted ancestors tonight declare
the children of Rafah tonight declare:
We did not knit blankets from hair braids
we did not spit on the face of murdered women
after plucking the golden teeth
Why do you take the candy
and give us bombs?
why make Arab children orphans?
And thanks?

Sadness turned us into men
we must fight

-2-

The sun was on a conqueror's bayonet
A naked hated corpse
bred silence on angry Muslim beds
flustered faces around it
an occupier with legendary features cried:
You will not speak?

fine—curfew
from this hour—
And from Aladdin's voice came
the birth of the birds of prey:
- I threw stones on the military vehicle
  I distributed pamphlets
  and gave the signal
  and painted slogans
  with a chair and a brush
  from a neighborhood to a house to a wall
  I gathered the children
and we swore by the refugee's exile
to resist
as long as a conqueror's bayonet
shines in our streets

Aladdin's age was no more
than ten years—
so knead tears and clay
if there is no flour
and cook sadness, patience and mud
in the name of the security of the conquerors
Oh wife of the man with unknown residence
What are you waiting for?
the joys of returning home on the safety bus
are lost—what are you waiting for?
lost—with all religions!

She asked her neighbor to care
for the son of the man with unknown residence
and She bought a red ticket
from the market of anger
and instead of a train in the station of safety
She took a train
climbing toward flaming stations!

An hour passed
and another hour
and an hour,
before She returned
on a bloody stretcher
Hana the brave

It is done,
do you have other relatives
in refugee tents
Oh son of the man with unknown residence
and son of the woman
who became impatient in safety stations
It is done

And like a wounded beast
the wind carried him
in his hand an idol
his father bought years ago from Jerusalem
on his way to Damascus
in Amman a Tunisian friend met him
visited Beirut
and spent a holiday in Cairo,
In his hand an idol
and the other hand an ink pot
made in Egypt
Like a wounded beast
carried by the wind

At the corner of the street
at the outskirts of town
the children of long histories
were gathering books, wood, and orphanage
frames and tent pegs
to build a barricade,

to block the path of darkness
and disturb the troops of hate
until peace washes their eyes
from the dust of hate and war!
And with books, wood, and orphanage
frames and tent pegs
his idol gave the barricade a nervous silence
and his hand was ready with the ink pot—

And the day the security doors of the conquerors closed
he was among the arrested
the son of the man whose residence was unknown

Footnote:
His age nine years—

FROM DIARIES OF A FIGHTER

When night falls
and the plain and hill sleeps
we leave our bases
the voice of the howling wolf
comforting us
we are hungry
searching like the wolf
for a hunt
The wolf might satisfy his hunger
but my comrades' hunger is eternal
because our hungry gun
will not be satisfied
with two or four sheep

We drew step by step
the plan for the night
some of us slept
and I thought back about my house
my poems
and Laila who came to bid farewell
"We will part
my heart will bleed
tomorrow the neighborhood will know
that you are in Palestine
and the relatives and friends will come
to congratulate us
and I shall live patiently
on the memory of our evenings
Do not forget
before fighting the battle
the twenty years
we spent in agony

and in bitter nights
we witnessed the birth of the revolution
We sat listening to the radio
the olive trees protecting us
and *Fairuz*'s voice
scourging us with songs:

My profession is sadness and waiting
waiting for that which never comes
the flowers of time have disappeared
for twenty years I
lived on sadness and hope"

Memory took me back
to past days
when we lived on your soil Oh Palestine
until Zion came with the devil
I swear by the dear blood
by hate that like fire
burns in my veins
by the martyrs before me
and after me
you will be frightened of the echo
of my voice
and you will remain all night
watching me

We heard a patrol
that appeared on the horizon
my comrades had waited all night
we changed our position
hail Zion
my mine is buried deep
I can see your vanity
as you approach inside a tank

so come we will with death
dig a hole in night
you believed in illusions
and were deceived oh Zion
for this is the land of my birth

I sucked its milk a child
and my grandfathers lived here
by God I will not rest
until war decides
my recitation is the gun
and the mines
and silent infiltration at night
followed by horror

either you Zion
or victory and the Arabs.

A HANGING HUMAN 1964

*One of the toys that appeared on the Israeli market was
that of a "hanged Arab."*

A hanging human body
The prettiest of toys
The sweetest recreation for children
Displayed on the market!
No, it is not there anymore
It has been sold out for days
Don't search for it, tell your child
It's sold out for days!

Oh, souls of those
Dead in Nazi concentration camps—
The hanged human
Is not a Jew in Berlin.
The hanged human is an Arab
Like me, of my people
Hanged by your brothers-
Forgive me, hanged by the crypto Nazis
In Zion!

Souls of the victims
Of Nazi camps—
If only you knew!
If only you knew!

THE HORSES

In distant lands
Infants are tiny
So light and glow
Overfill their days
The tale of the sun
They tell them in lines
So the little child
Becomes a man—a great man

In our land
The infant prince
So might and vows
Pour upon his eyes
And on his delicate skin
Castles are built
So the *princely* child
Becomes a dwarf—a little man
He swallows mud
And crunches fruit rind

In distant lands
The child grows up
And with him the qualities evolve
And stars and hopes unroll upon his brow
In our land—
Among the rings of smoke the child grows
And so they say: "A woman's dream is Heaven's guard"
Or "A bridegroom—He is of age."

So stock of bridegrooms floods our land
A generation of monstrous children—like horses
Their heads are filled with color-less reflection

Should my people breed the child as a child
They would not toss mud in his eyes
Perhaps on our land there would shine
A generation of knights—in my country

And children would be born as little ones
Later they become men and fill the night with fire
Perhaps I might view an eagle around
Not birds imitating eagles

In other lands
People are concerned about the end result
In our land
People are worried about the beginning
That the wife should bear a male child
So they could say: "She's of noble stock"
She bore a boy
Whose face is like the moon's
So they would say: "Her husband is a stud-
horse—he's a man".
Or "an Arab steed—invincible hero
His firstborn is a male
Whose face is like the moon's"
But then the sow becomes a shepherd of flies,
A worm of the earth and its dust
He may be dumb—blind—an owl in a ruin
Though his father die and though his mother die
And though she died from the thrill of birth
It is sufficient he is born a male
Whose face is like the moon's
His mother of eminent breed—
A mare that does not falter
Her husband a thorough-bred stallion—
A triumphant hero

My country—tell me when, o my country
When will you smother us with light, not with slumber
As you have smothered us in home and milk
So may the slave market be destroyed
And the block horses jump in the fire
So when the flocks of birds enclose
Behold they are falcons and eagles.

IN ENEMY LINES

Yesterday, he stopped me in the street, asked about a
    bar
Where he could pass the evening.
He was a black sailor,
A deck-hand in a ship of the Dollar,
We talked, and I liked him
Would you like a drink, friend?
At a secluded table in the noisy cafe
My friend drank heedlessly
This black man wanted to forget
Why? from what depths does this man spring?
Tell me of your life in America the free,
Of the white man's school, of his church, and his hotel
Speak to me of the fluorescent signs:
No dogs, Jews, or Negroes allowed!
"Oh leave me alone for Satan's sake
Is there a woman around? Before dawn
We'll be sailing and leaving this port!"
Very well! Tell me of the land of the black fire
Have you heard of a hunted lion?
Of the forests becoming ashes in the night
Of a field planted with martyrs
Of a people grown in a land
Watered with the blood of the murdered
Of a sun born pregnant with bread, dreams and free-
    dom?
Have you heard of Africa?
"I hear, I hear, the rolls of the Simbas' drums
I see a black beauty
Writhing like an angry fire
In a dance of bloodied love."
Very well! Speak to me of Cuba.

What do you know of a people that are
No longer a crucified Christ.
"Cuba? If I had a guitar tonight
If I sing a song
A curtain would move and reveal
A sensuous body in the window."
"Waitress!
Damn you, my glass is empty.
And my senses are still clear, and the entertainer
What silenced his tunes?"
Yesterday he stopped me in the street
Searching for a bar
This morning the news told of
A white American who died,
As his lips quivered with a cry:
Down with the words
Written in blood, in anguish,
Down with the shame of man
Raised by the Fascists waving mud-stained banners
Those words that say:
No dogs, Jews, or Negroes allowed.

ON AMERICAN INDIANS

Flowers on the graves, America,
And dancing and songs on the remains—
There is nothing left but films
Films that make you laugh and cry,
My dead brothers, it is funny and tearful.
The farms of the colonists stretch across the prairie
Large, green, and fertile.
The noisy factories of the colonists' heirs destroy the
    earth
And pollute the sky—
What shall I say, brothers?
Alas for your history!
And death for a civilization that lives
On destruction—and blood.

THE UNKNOWN CONTINENT

How do we reach you
Slums of Chicago?
How is the spark to reach you?
How is the fire to be born?
Skyscrapers!
Stacked huts!
Stretch your arms out of the darkness—
For the big banner
Spreads its warmth, its light
Forever
Into the depths of night
And the big banner is
Forever
A sail for the drowning.

How are the storms to reach you

Jazzband Club in New York?
The blackman is hungry and fearful,
The wolves of the KKK roam the forest
—the current overpowering
And the conscience of the *statue* shaken
And the heart of night.
The wind is frozen,
And the waves of the sea unmoving?
How is the message to reach you
Deaf Washington,
With the humming of the machine?
In Vietnam slaughter,
And you export
Cokes and medicine to the sad moon!

And you sweep over the blood of victims.
How is the message to reach you?

Descendants of Old Abe!
My voice has become hoarse
And the wind
Has become tired of my shouts!

Descendants of Old Abe!
Shake the marble of history,
Rise to the sky,
Rise above the band of stupid magis
And halt- for
The earth grumbles
The rivers of blood.

THUNDERBIRD

In the land called the *United States of America* there lives a tribe of red indians called *Zuni*. It is said that this tribe awaits the coming of a holy bird, whose wings cause thunderbolts and streaks of lightning when they touch the horizon, bringing goodness, accompanied by freedom, roses, and food. The *Zunis* call their awaited bird *Thunderbird*. They tattoo his image on their chests and embroider it on their children's blankets, and their spears.

It will be that he shall come
He shall come with the sun
A face disfigured with the dust of the learning path
It will be that there shall come
After the suicide of drought, in my voice
Something—of unlimited wonders
Something that was called in the song:
Thunderbird!

No doubt he shall come
For we have reached it,
Reached the peak of death.

FROM THE DIARY OF JOHNNY GUITAR

Johnny was not meant for war, but for love and the guitar. He was drafted by President Lyndon Johnson and dispatched to Vietnam. While in the front lines, Johnny kept a diary— addressing his beloved who earned her living by working in a napalm factory—awaiting Johnny's return—her darling, Johnny Guitar.

— 1 —

In the dingy swamp
With snakes and alligators
My story begins:
My path to sin
Prepare my food
Clothings and guitar
And my poem book

—2—

I dip my hair
In ink, my darling
To declare mourning
On my waxy forehead
And from within my tears
I continue singing
To my love back home
To your crying face
Expressing farewell
Like a winter's flower—
May the President commiserate
Any may the heavens have mercy
On your lovely face
Any bring near my return

—3—

I was barred from carrying my guitar
In the heart of battle
And while a tune walked to me
From a world destroyed
My fingers trembled
Because, my darling, your wretched musician
Did not excel in playing the machine gun

—4—

I've cheated you in my dreams
I fell in love, my darling
But not for real
A girl came down from the north
Her name is unknown to me
But I cried, my darling
Because in the battle field
I was—her enemy!

—5—

And on Christmas Eve
I was asked to play
And sing
In a hall with falling walls
And flames dancing inside—
Its floor is covered with blood
Ashes, and corpses of boys

It was an order, my darling!

—6—

The morning was glorious
In the jungle of traps

But my *buddy* Mike was lonely and sad
He is a dancer, comical and gay
Mike is a Negro from the South
His brother arrived with a new platoon
Leaving his mother in a shock in Detroit
A widow, lonely, and depressed
He said, my darling,
His father was mutilated in a riot!

My *buddy* Mike was desolate and grave

The morning was glorious
In the jungle of traps
But the day was miserable
In the jungle of traps-
When I saw Mike fall to the ground
With a red forehead!
The silence exploded
And suddenly I felt a sting
In the chest—on the left
Where I kept your face and my guitar
And later I woke up on a stretcher.
Prepare the flowers and the tears
So they may say to me - if I returned alive-
You have come back, hurrah! hurrah!
Or if I returned in a wooden box-
Which you may have filled with napalm one day-
They may be relatives at the airport
Receiving my body from the aeroplane.

FROM VIETNAM

*(This poem was inspired by an address of the delegate of the
Vietnamese National Liberation Front delivered in Amman on the
occasion of the Jerusalem Day)*

His Eastern face appeared lightsome
Like the dawn
His slender figure was tenacious
Like a spear
He came on the Day of Jerusalem
To give an account
It livened our hearts
His words uttered triumph
And the joy of struggle
His eyes reflected defeat of the Fleet
And the aircraft carriers
Helpless in the sea
His arm was stiffened
His heart unyielding
He crushed the intruder
And inflicted wounds
His temperament is gentle—
But not in war
The doctrine of liberation—
Knows no reprieve

He said: In Vietnam,
The land of earthquakes
We cross our path
On the light of torch
Sometime ago, I lived on the land
Free of war
Seeding the plain

Awaiting the harvest
But the greedy came—
To invade my home
And suddenly,
The morning saw a flood of bombs
A wicked enemy with power replete
In the air, land, and in the sea

He opened fire
And waved his dollars
To buy a friend
Naive he is
To think that faith can go on sale
Or to think that torture and raid
Can deter free men
Neither the rockets
Nor the incursions
Destroyed our souls
We laid a bridge
From our nerves
To get the caravans
On their way

The man declared: Long line experiments
Revolutions of free men
Will conquer usurpers
The assaults of America
And her Israel
Do not dispirit fighting men
We built a trench,
It's our home
The home of glory
In the flames of war.

O messenger of the east
You are a splendid messenger
O sun of the East
Do not ever set
O enemy of deception
We are alike
In mind and heart
We are the east
Whose sun is lofty
And every injustice
Inflicting the East
Will wither away

May the steps of your heroes be blessed
O brother
We sow the seeds of triumph
On these plains
And watered the hills
With precious blood
The state of oppression
Will soon decay.

LORCA

Lorca!
Forgive the flowering of the blood
The sun is in your hands—a cross
Bearing poetic fire.
The handsomest of youths travel to you
A martyr, and a martyress.

Thus is the poet
An earthquake, a flood of water
And storms if he reared.
One street stone whispered to the other:
He has passed by so fly oh stone.

Thus is the poet, music, and prayer chants
And a breeze if he whispers, and
Takes the maid with the gentility of the gods.
And the moons are his nest
If he wishes to sleep.

Espagna remains a sad mother.
Letting her hair down on her shoulders.
On the blackened olive branches
She hung her swords.

The guitar player roams the streets
At night singing your songs - in secret -
Oh *Lorca,* and collecting handouts
From the eyes of the wretched.

The black eyes in *Espagna* glance wearily
And the conversations of love are muted

And the poet digs his grave
If he opens his mouth.

Forgetfulness forget to walk in your steps
The reflected smiles of the moon are covered with your
    blood
And the noblest of swords is a word from your lips
On the songs of gypsies.

Most beautiful among the lands is *Espagna,* and *Lorca*
Is the handsomest of youth - oh maidens,
Singer of fire! Distribute your embers to the millions
We worship the flame.

In the last bulletin from Madrid, the wound cried:
The patient one has had his fill of patience,
They executed Julian at night, and the orange blossoms
Continue to spread their aroma.

The most beautiful news from Madrid
Will come tomorrow.

CUBA

1

My friends in the fertile sugar fields
My friends in the oil refineries in proud Cuba-
From my village, my precious home
I send you greetings:
Scented kisses—delicious boxes of sweets
I have for you bouquets of flowers
And songs of magic—the chirping of the birds
I wish I had wings—like an eagle
To carry these gifts.

2

The people of my village tell of many stories
About you,
They tell them proudly—with glowing eyes
With hearts beaming with joy and jealousy
On the golden hills they gather, at high noon,
Under the trees, in the pastures, in the humble lanes
Their conversation is a medley of fire and May, a moving
        song.
The people in my land love the truly heroic.
My friends who have filled the world with the fragrance
        of struggle
Keep up the pressure on the imperialists
They have cut my wings.
Within me lies the vengeance of a wounded people
Thrown into the streets
A people yearning for their usurped lands
Press on—the wings of the eagle are stronger
Than the hurricanes,
The imperialists do not understand

The language of humility and tears
They only understand the people surge
To the arena of struggle.

PATRICE LUMUMBA

"The poet of freedom and its messenger in the jungles of the Congo."

Beat the wind and soar
Oh rebellious lover of freedom
O you eagle repelled by existence
In a humiliated, shackled valley.
As you twisted in the cesspool of mud and thorns
Fired by a yearning for light
And your dreams gleamed with the visions
Of Jesus, Moses, and the aspirations of Muhammad.
Illuminating a craving for lofty summit
Soaring among the stars in the far beyond.
You pranced for glory, your faraway haven
That perches on deep-seated dignity.

O you cheers whose tremors
Rocked the sad, tormented Congo
Hoodwinked by a gang that slave-drove
The people and delivered them to a foreign master
O great eagle of Africa, the calling of the sun
Looms and thunders in the universe.
And it was you who heeded its appeal, cried:
Mother, I heed, And tomorrow we *rendezvous*
On the horizon of heroic gallantries.
You braced your wings, your beak throbbing with flames
Your tears restrained.
And you glittered, a star breaking
The long drawn screen of darkness.
So—carry the magnificent torch and
Dispel the reign of night that the invaders
Wanted to be eternal, perpetual.

AFTER THE JUNE AGGRESSION

What did you hide
for to-morrow
You shed my blood
and dimmed the light
of my eyes
You silenced my pen
and usurped the right
of peaceful men
who did not sin

What did you hide
for to-morrow
you rent my flag
and opened wounds
in my skin
You stabbed my dreams
What do you hide?

We're deeper than the sea
and taller than the stars
Our breath is long
longer than space

Which mother, I wonder
inherited you half the Canal
Which mother
inherited you the Jordan Bank
the sand, petroleum, and the Heights
He who forcibly takes a right
must guard his own
When the balance shifts

ON THE FIFTH OF JUNE

On the fifth,
Of June last
We returned to death its diplomatic bags
On the fifth
Of June last
We stripped the western winds
Of its ornamentation
Polished by children's blood
And by the shame of ruins
On the fifth
Of June last
The dead ascended to the United Nations
To partake in the emergency meeting
On the fifth
Of June last
We viewed the whole face of the globe
On the fifth
Of June last
The Arab oil wells continued flowing
In the midst of Arab lands
Towards the soil of western winds
On the fifth
Of June last

I do not weep!
I do not smile!

FAREWELL IN SOPHIA

Do not say farewell
Tomorrow we shall meet
Twenty years ago
My father told me:
"A tragedy is a sail!"

Therefore, I didn't sell my boat
Therefore, do not say good bye
Tomorrow we shall meet!

IT OCCURRED ON THE FIFTH OF JUNE

The reader may or may not recall
What we often said in village halls

The reader may or may not recall
But we said it repeatedly
In precise and sound words

The lightning which strikes in the road
Provides the passer-by with light
Despite the burns

The reader may or may not remember
But so that everyone will know
I repeat!

We are in the Fifth
Of the month of June
We're born anew.

RESIGNATION FROM THE LIFE INSURANCE COMPANY

(About those who began to think after the fifth of June)

Ladies, and gentlemen!
I am a humble citizen
I offer my resignation
To the company's manager
This is my identity card
Honored by his signature
Ladies and gentlemen!
I submit my resignation
From a rotten vocation
Burdensome on the conscience
Let my name be recorded
In the register of the exasperated!
Who ceased to dance in the graveyard
And believed in the sun and man
Who preferred the earth!
Ladies, and gentlemen!
We are here
At the point of cross-roads
Let he who wants to drown, drown
Let him mount unbroken horses
If this is his choice
If I am asked which path is mine
It is the left—my path
That of the sun—and the left
      the wheat—and the left
      the tears—and the left
The path of death
Until the orbit of the globe
      moves to the left.

LETTER TO A WOMAN

I waited for you—but, you were not born yet!
And the train is tooting, ready to pull out.
The train has learned from Man:
>   *Not to be patient and not to have time!*
And you are not yet born,
>   And the train wants to start
>   I'm sorry,
>   I have to board!

But I'm leaving this letter
In the cafe near the station.
When you get here, take a seat and ask for coffee,
Black coffee with *white* milk,
They'll make a strange combination, the two colors,
Like the color of modern man's heart.

Then ask the waitress:
"Didn't he leave a letter for me?"
And she won't understand—But perhaps she'll answer
    crossly:
"Everyone leaves letters here for everybody!
And all the letters say the same thing:
'I love you, because I love me'!"

Then go to the kitchen and see the cook;
My letter may have gone to her for cooking;
And she may well say to you:
"In the soup I once found
A slip of paper that said:
>   'Darling,
>   They've sent me to die for my country;
>   You - you try and live for us!'"

Then go to the cafe owner;
It is possible that the letter was lost
Among his bills and receipts;
It is also possible that he will hand you
A menu saying:

> For half a pound: You get a cup of coffee
> For a pound: You get a bottle of beer
> For a human being: Only thirst!

Then leave the cafe!
Look no further for my letter,
For selections of it have already reached you -
Each section from someone else!

I'm very glad that these sections
Will reach you after you've been born,
For I think that if my letter had reached you
Before you were born
You would have preferred not

> To be born in this century,
> And that would be a loss.

THE BATS

The bats on the window
swallow my voice,
The bats at my door
And the bats behind the papers.
In the corners,
Follow my steps, and my glances.
The bats on the seat,
In the street, behind me,
On the window pane of the bookstore,
on the girls legs.
And I look back.

The bats are on my neighbor's window
The bats are receivers hidden in a wall
The bats are about to commit suicide.

I continue on my way towards the daylight.

THE LAND OF THE SEVENTY WONDERS

Grief is jasmine
In the land of the seventy wonders
And poverty is music
And the death of God in an ambush
Is bread,
And the learned professor of languages
Jurisprudence and medicine
Is *Juha's ass*—And grief is jasmine
In the land of seventy wonders!

الاستعمار ينقض على فلسطين

MY HOMELAND

(Written from prison after the June 1967 war)

My Homeland:
The chains have taught me
The fierceness of the eagle
And the tenderness of the optimist
I did not know
That under our skin
A storm is being born
And rivers are being wed.
They dimmed the light in my prison cell
But a radiant sun is beaming in my heart
They wrote my number on the wall
And a plain of wheat has grown
I carved your bloody picture with my teeth
And wrote a song for the dying night
I stabbed my defeat in the flesh of dark
And stitched my fingers in the verse of light
While the conqueror stands on the roof of my home
He only conquered my cell
He only saw my glow
He only heard my chains
And if I am burnt on the cross of prayers
I shall become a saint—dressed in a uniform

ON HOPE

Do not tell me:
I wish to be a baker in Algeria
In order to sing with the revolutionaries
Do not tell me:
I wish to be a shepherd in the Yemen
To sing for the uprising of the age
Do not tell me:
I wish to be a waiter in Havana
To sing for the victory of the poor
Do not tell me:
I wish to be a stone carrier in Aswan
To sing for the rocks
My friends:
The Nile will not pour into the Volga
The Congo and Jordan Rivers
Will not serve the Euphrates
Each river has its own
Our land is not barren
Each land has its own rebirth
Each dawn has a date with revolution.

A DATE WITH THE RAIN

Strike—your hands are of steel!
Strike—you are the only command giver
And we, master,
Who are we? rather—
What are we,
But a handful of slaves!
Strike!
Trample on the slaves' dignity,
Strike—you are the command giver in our land,
Forgive me, I should say
In your land
In your far-flung land where you planted roses
That the world may see them
From afar, whenever you wish
And praise the master in the promised land.

Strike,
Put whomever you wish
In the cell of death
And if you desire, master
The sheep will march in humility—without regret
For you are our fate and destiny
You do as you wish
Changing our ages carelessly
Does someone like you fear men?
Forgive me—remnants of men!
And you, in your height, the command giver?

Strike—your arms are of steel
And we thank you,
Your illustrious whip
Taught us stubbornness in the face of the ages.

We have come to shake the balance of crisis
Our life has become a resolution,
Our thanks to you—
You taught us to stand up.

Despite your tyranny
Despite your Fascist terror
Never mind it all!
Our flesh is a bridge
On the stormy seas
A bridge
To banks that never betrayed us
Or we never betrayed them.

Bury your dead and arise
Even if the morrow could fly
It shall not escape us.
We were crushed
But formed anew.

the case

i want a gun
my mother's ring, i sold
to buy a gun
my pocketbook, i pledged
and recorded accounts
to buy a gun

the language we studied
the books we read
the poems we recited
are not worthwhile
compared to a gun

i now have a gun
to Palestine, take me with you
to the gloomy hills
like the face of the Virgin
to the greenslopes
and the sacred stones, take me with you

twenty years have passed away
while i still search for land
and identity
i searched for my house, over there
i searched for my Homeland
it is encamped and circled with wire
i searched for the bike
and for my friends
i searched for my books and photographs
and for every warm spot and every vase

to Palestine, take me with you
i want to live—or die
like a man
i want to flourish in the soil
like an olive tree
or an orange grove
or a fragrant flower

i now have a gun
tell the curious about my case
my gun—has now become the case

i now have a gun
i'm in the roster of the commandos
i sleep on thorns and dust
and speak to death
my weapons grow leaves
and my wounds reflect the moon
and the sun rises—

my will is hard like a rock
and my fist is a tornado
a fatalist, i am not
my destiny, i shape
i'm one of the freedom fighters
i'm one of them
since i carried my gun
Palestine is near

oh revolutionaries
In Jerusalem, Hebron, Beisan
and the Aghwar

in Bethlehem—where once you were free
pour out like rain
and multiply
like grass and flowers
advance—advance—
the story of peace
is only a play

THE ARAB

I've lost my shadow!
How tragic!
No sun, no moon, no stars,
I am not here, nor there!
An unperson lost nowhere.
It's cool, dank and musty,
All around me, no one knows me.
No one cares.
And no person, no roots no trunks no branches.
The wind thrashes me about,
The sun, I never see.
And the gentle breeze shakes me.
Under a microscope in the tents where I live.
My house is not a house,
My tent has no shadow, no foundation,
No root.
Some people. Most do not,
No one really cares.
For, I have lost my shadow,
My history is gone,
My present bleak,
My future bloody,
The only glow, the only hope,
Red, crimson red, comes liberation.

REMARKS ABOUT THE AGGRESSION (1967)

On the edge of the pond
dark clouds
children and wheat
wasting dew.
Graves,
the passage of days
will not guarantee
a martyr
With tank chains
on his dark forehead.
"We have won" Ha!
A magician
gave the signal
last breath
and the light
of my eyes
made
open wounds.
In my skin
dreams
hide a
deeper water
higher than the stars.
The balance shifts.
What else can happen?
Earth, tell us,
conqueror
pregnant
with cotton and mud

ON THE TRUNK OF AN OLIVE TREE

In the courtyard
I shall carve my story:
tragic chapters end
sighs near the graves
of my dead.
Because I cannot knit the tail,
my house is exposed to visitation,
inspection and "expurgation."
I engrave every secret
in an olive tree,
and carve the bitterness I tasted
after the sweetness of love.
"Kafr Qassim,
I shall never forget thee."
"Deir Yassin's memory
is spreading roots."
"We reached the climax
of the tragedy." Words!
I shall carve
the sun
and the moon
and whatever the lark sings
on that olive tree
in the courtyard of the house.

IS IT ENOUGH?

Earth, grass, flowers,
—Is it enough?
This year's equinox
collides
with the wailing
rabbits
praying in
shadows
of urban renewal.
All the year's
joy
is downtown.
The Ides
bring
the tides of
supply and demand.
Salt and oil and
Jesus
Moses, Muhammad,
and sand.
Jerusalem is a
holy ménage à
trois.
Is it enough?

SHELTER NO. 20

Our songs were like the empty day
of soldiers returning from battle
and like the loneliness
of the tubercular patient
coughing in the night,
and we wandered without shadows
awaiting the night,
The news brought in the mail:
"Shelter No. 20. We are still well,
The family, the lice, and the dead
send greetings to our relatives."
And the unripe, deformed memories go by,
And the tents, the wind, the day and the night.
Like our faces after the exodus:
"Mother, we are still well."
And the wolves howl
Across the desert of sleeplessness.
My brothers, where do we begin? From here.
From the high of coughing
and our returning tearful mail,

"Nothing is remembered.
Yafa is still there, and so are the compatriots
Swinging headless in the air under the bridges
and above the pillars of light.
And our spilled blood is still there
on its old walls, and the thieves,
and our bare fields are invaded by locusts."
From here, mother, came the wood
for the scaffolds and the fire
From here they came, and we come.
The road is long and rocky

and the cowards and the meek
do not deserve to live

Yafa, we shall return to you tomorrow
during the harvest season
with the swallows and the spring
with the compatriots returning from exile, from prison
with the forenoon and the skylarks
with the mothers.
Shelter No. 20:
"The family is still well
And your brothers, displaced from our lost
home send greetings to the relatives."

BARBED WIRE

The shouts of the vineyard guard
awaken me at night
And I hear the howling
of the north wind
in the olive grove repeating,
in my ears, the tragedy of
my defeated people,
my steadfast people,
the tragedy of loss.
And it is as if a battle rages
silently, sadly and insistently,
Between me and death.
I shall not die as long as
there is oil in the lamps
of the refugee nights
and fire across the border graveyard
where old tents stand
stand like a sign in the wind
pointing to the bloody road of return.

TO MY MOTHER

Do not brood
For I shall forget your sad face
In the joy of the struggle,
And the agonies of those eyes
And the size of those wrinkles
I shall forget
When the battle rages
Do not worry
For I have a goal in death.
I shall embrace it with my eyes
And I shall walk to my aim
With the patience of a prophet
With the eye of a prophet
So that I may reach it
During the joy of the battle.

Do not brood
For the wounds of my life in my chest
Pain me
And the call of fate
Colors my life with vengeance
And pushes me toward danger
And lives in agonies in my mind
And sews me to the stirrup
And I walk to my death
And my pride marches with me
And on my way march the wounds of youth,
So do not block the desires that are in my eyes.
Your tears are a blasphemy
You shall not weaken me
And you shall not keep me from going
For our rights call me to battle,

To glory, so that I may reach it.
I have crucified my destiny there
Along the mountain passes.
I see it milling, singing,
Waving among the banners
My destiny, and your destiny
And among the spears (or the bayonets) and this road

MY SON KAMAL

Those who knew Kamal Nasser closely knew the extent of his closeness to his mother. To him she was the land and the sweetheart, the sister and the mother—the constant yearning. The following poem by Wadi'a Nasser appeared after her son's murder in the Arabic Newspaper in Jerusalem, The Dawn. *The poem appeared on the front page of the paper along with a picture of Kamal and led to the swift arrest of the owner and editors of* The Dawn *and to a temporary ban of the paper.*

My son Kamal:
They prevented my eyes from seeing you
Being placed in the earth
They thought that I could not see you.
I see you in every youth
I hear your steps marching insistently:
"I shall not die today
I am a revolutionary
My road is the road of revolutionaries
My death shakes the fire
My death inflames the fire
My people live today."

My son Kamal:
I am a mother who raised a man who said:
"Do not brood
For the wounds of my life in my breast
Pain me
And the call of fate
Colors my life with vengeance
And pushes me toward danger."

You ask me not to mind
And you know that I am a mother
I love you, oh part of myself, (flesh of my flesh, heart of
    my heart, oh child of mine?)
But your love for your land is deeper than all loves
And that is why my pride in you shakes my being
For I am the mother of him who has given himself
Who said:
"Your tears are a blasphemy
You shall not weaken me
And you shall not keep me from going
For our rights call me to battle,
To glory, so that I may reach it"*

My destiny,
Your destiny is among the bayonets
Your destiny is a symbol to all youth
Your destiny is proud and they shall not defeat me,
They shall not weaken me.
With the strength of action
I shall continue to hear your voice see you in every youth
And I shall continue to hear your voice
In the mountain passes
Shouting:
"We shall remain in spite of the enemy
In death, we shall be resurrected anew
And we shall raise our banner proudly."

---

* Lines from Kamal Nasser's poem "To My Mother" are quoted here.

THE HOUSE

The house
Like those who were here
The house whispers about guidance
There is no one
They closed the windows
And fled
They took a whole life with them
And what remains is
The shadow voice on the walls of distance
The door remains and so does the shattered echo
And their footsteps that we used to hear next to the door
Declare
From here, they've disappeared
And yet, they remained
And they disappeared like a rose
ripped from the heart of the earth
And yet,
its fragrant scent fills the air
Descending
And a sound like silence is heard descending on the stairs
Like a wailing wound
And tears falling on the tiles

THE MASSACRED VILLAGE

Blood, blood, blood
As if the Earth does not grow grass
Now without blood.
And the flesh on flesh
And the blood
Heightens the beastly desires
For destruction.
And the little ones huddle,
Frightened
Amid the dust and the fire
As if the black daggers
Had caught off their mother's breasts
Before them.
Their mother's breasts,
Their milk
And they gasp "water,"
From whom?
From heaven, little ones?
Even the doves flew from the hell of flames
Of fire
Even the doves fled

THEY TAUGHT ME

They taught me in school
Reading, writing and arithmetic
They taught me history and literature
How to pray and fast
I observe the sun
The moon and the stars
I am blessed from kissing the earth
And kissing the olive trees
In the Holy Land
Thus, they taught me in school
Jerusalem: the birthplace of religions
In it, Christ was crucified
And rose after he died
And Muhammad walked to it and ascended to the high
    heavens
Abraham gave birth to the descendants of Solomon
Palestine the birthplace of religions
In the Holy Land
That's what the school has taught me
Wow! What I've learned.
I learned afterwards

That religion is bought and sold on the New York Stock
    Exchange
In the halls/pathways of the Vatican
And the religious leaders and the kings and the presidents
Seek blessing in silence
Their hands are tied
The children shout: "Victory is coming, cowards."
The revolution of the people is mighty
The weapons of these children are stones
The bombs of the revolutionaries are sparks
That is what the school of life has taught me

PRISONERS

The sun pierces through the railing
Her warmth defies my darkness
She beats down the walls that hold me
Every morning as she rises
In every dream, she makes her entry
And of hope and life, reminds me.

My children stand distant but I can see them
Peering their gentle faces through the glass
Words and tears mix with apprehension
But their smiles are gesturing embraces
Their eyes starve for my affection
For a while, I bask in their attention

My mother waits alone for the harvest
The olive trees have kept their promises
And yield their bounty to her picking
Filling her now heavy baskets
She collects my fears and aches
And tends to everything in her keeping

The jasmine's perfume exposes an escape
From my occupier's jail to my mother's table
The stars collude with my senses
Like Aladdin's magic carpet, I become the stuff of fables
To fly over electric walls and barbed fences
Above the hate and lost innocence

By years of confinement, I should be hardened
From my torturer's whips, I should be weary
From the loneliness, I should be silent
But freedom never has a sentry
When despair hollows my hopes for an instant
My motherland comes to my nourishment

WHEN I BECAME MY MOTHER'S DAUGHTER

I became my mother's daughter
Not when I emerged from her womb and gasped my
    first breath
Not when I tiptoed from under her shadow and took my
    own steps
Not when I lined my eyes with Kohl and called myself a
    woman
Or draped her colors on every memory of her I still held
That did not make me her daughter yet

When the soil of Palestine nourished the seeds of my
    thoughts
The heaviness of a history sinking under old cobbled roads
I found the old steel doors of the Old City ready to confess
Secrets sealed between its scarred contours and depths
Like exquisite butterflies I make them my own

We dipped our bread, she and I, in *za'atar* and olive oil
Planted the lemon tree in our gardens to remind us of
    home
And sipped an over-sweetened Turkish coffee under an
    alien sun
Lamenting the legends of ancestors to whom we once
    belonged
But that too did not make me her daughter yet

Her fingers strummed each worry bead to the hours of
    the night
And a weary mind that lingered in the shadows of the light
Twisting knives struck those old bones
She cursed growing gray in the shadow of walls
Bid the witness close her eyes and leave her alone

I became my mother's daughter
Not when I emerged from her womb and gasped my
    first breath
Not because we were made of the same blood and flesh
I became her daughter when
My feet sank into her footprints
My eyes wept for her visions
My rage was stoked by the same fires
I became her daughter when
My bones and sinews twitched for Palestine without her
My words and thoughts lived outside of her
Months and then years, after she left.

HARAM ALAIKUM (SHAME ON YOU),
IT IS FORBIDDEN

Has the ocean not become parched from the salt of a
    mother's tears
A long-awaited child buried within one year
And the blessings of her life crushed into smithereens
Haram Alaikum. Wallah Haram
Have you seen her face glowing as though an angel
She wraps her prayers with rantings, her sobbing with
    laughter
Her praises with curses as the living become martyrs

Haram Alaikum. Wallah Haram

What of the newest lunatic from yesterday's prisons
His mind mangled with sinister visions
Have you seen the frozen stare of an unwilling witness

Are the orphans not most treasured for being the most
    wretched,
Do you not see them shaking like leaves at every rain drop
Roaming the streets, their feet cracked and blistered

Haram Alaikum, Wallah Haram

The soil is heavy with our bones
Do you not hear the groans of the dead from every
    crevice and clump
Under slab a fading heart
Lift it and find the voice of a child
And my words lie next to her as she cries

Haram Alaikum, Wallah Haram

DESPAIR IS THE ENEMY OF HUMANKIND
LOVE IS THE WAY TO GOD

Everyone on earth is a guest, no one lived forever after all
We will leave everything behind at the departure of the soul
Only our good deeds go up with us to heaven nothing more
We have to help each other and clearly define our goals
We should work together and support justice and peace
As both are like Siamese twins, living together side by side
Greet Pope Francis for asking all to open hearts and doors
And greet everyone supporting victims of terror and war

A MESSAGE OF PEACE

We are all children of Adam and Eve
We should not quarrel and fight
Should all strive to support love and peace
This message is in every religion
God wants us to live in peace and harmony
God is just. God is righteous.
Justice is the bridge to peace
Injustice and greed cause
Suffering and pain
They create conflict and war
They lead to the destruction
Of mankind and the homeland
Killing one soul is like killing all
God is forgiving and passionate
We are all guests in this world
Though we have different circumstances
We all came from clay
God created us and loves us all
And to live happy and safe
We need to support and maintain peace
Peace is one of God's glorious names
God is merciful, God is great

FLOOD (OCTOBER 2023)

Like the sun and moon
Verses of night and day are drawn
Emitting constantly
Like the heavens and earth
Mirrors of the eye and the heart
spread
Witnesses
Like the sea and river
A flood overflows
Far eastern winds
Carrying all the names
Glory be to my Creator, the Initiator
& Evolver

IMPRINTS ĠAZZÄ (FALL 2024)

faces and their names
engrave rain clouds
carve stones
with their blood
the sea, land and air
mix
with their veins,
flesh, bones, and the last breath
worlds wake up
wills sustain
water nourishes
their souls and pains
taken in vain

memory inflames
beating hearts
buried bodies
amputated bodies
decomposed bodies
evaporated bodies
shredded bodies
young and old bodies
rise

Friday, 30 August, 2024

THE ANTHEM OF RETURN

My brother,
No matter how dark the night is,
We will see the dawn
No matter how much poverty subdues, tomorrow we
    will abase it
My brother, the black tent has become our grave
Tomorrow we will turn it into a garden and build a
    palace over it
The cry of the free will rise on the day of return
And the bells of terror will pass, whether on land or at
    sea

IMMORTAL SEA, YOUR SEA

To my father

You taught me how to hold the fishing rod,
feel the tugs, and it took all of my small body
to hold onto you and the rod as we stood
on the Beirut shore. Sometimes you would choose
a spot on the slippery rocks that jutted out to sea,
to get closer to the bass and bream.
Those days I learned what *sabr** was,
watching you take in the unending distances
with your eyes, the patience of waiting.

There was tenderness in your casting dance,
a longing as you moved your body
toward the horizon. A line of poetry would often
emerge from your lips— something about how to live
with dignity, search for pearls in the sea,
appreciate the power of the pen over the sword.
It seemed on those days that whether the fish
found you didn't matter.

Had you had your way
with what your life should have been like
without the war, the Mediterranean
would have been the cradle of everything
you dreamed. You taught all of us to swim,
to submerge our heads, not to be afraid
of the salt and the vast airless space.
I was hypnotized by the motion
of your arms as you swam in the depths
parallel to shore, following a line

---

* *Sabr* is the Arabic word for patience.

that was infinite yet close.
In Haifa you had owned ships and traded
in cargo between the countries that shared
the same expanse of blue—until the world war
halted your dreams. Then the Nakba
put your relatives on boats going northward
and it was the Mediterranean, again,
that witnessed your woes.
The sea became the archive of your losses.

So when we moved to Beirut, you tried
to reimagine it—as a chronicler, a place
of reflection, wondrous and generous and deep.
It was where you could bring your family
to picnic and frolic on Sundays,
dig in the sand to reach the water below.
You could invoke the other meaning
of sea, the bahr that refers to meter
in classical Arab poetry, a lovely convergence.
You relished reciting the couplets of Al-Mutanabbi*
and Shawqi, but later with our beloved Darweesh,
you saw the bahr ebbing, the structure
giving way to unrhymed free verse:
your history unhinged, taken apart, regrouped.

Maybe we should have scattered your ashes
over the sea, the poetry of your being
going back to where it belongs.
You would have been one with the fish
and the boats, the rocks and sand and waves,
sabr, memories, and loss. We could have
then visited you and touched Palestine
everywhere, in your immortal sea.

---

* Al-Mutanabbi is one of the greatest Arab poets who lived during the tenth century.

A SINGLE SENTENCE

*The Palestinian struggle . . . can be summarized in a single
sentence: we are here, we belong, we are human, we deserve
equality and freedom.*
—*Tweet by Ussama Makdisi, 5/13/2021*

We Are Here

All my grandparents were born in Nazareth.
And their parents and grandparents
and great grandparents
before them.
My maternal Jiddi Amin and Sitti Olga
and my paternal Jiddi Salim and Sitti Roumieh
had nine children between them
who went on to have twenty-eight more.

We continue to birth new generations of Palestinians.
We are self-replenishing olive trees with hard trunks.
We have long, stubborn roots.
We are here.

We Belong

Like white blossoms dotting the almond tree
Like the vibrant redness of a poppy flower
Like the rings of Saturn, the moon's pull to earth
Like the flickering heartbeat of the stars
Like the morning trill of the goldfinch
Like the water ripple that first cleaves to a central ring,
moves outward then calms and returns
—as we return.
We belong.

We Are Human

Fingers and arms, legs and feet
Heads that contemplate, hearts that plead
Lungs that breathe teargas
Flesh that meets bullets
We bleed, we bleed

Need we prove more?
We are human.

We Deserve Equality and Freedom

We are here.
We belong.
We are human.
We deserve equality and freedom.

COLORS FOR THE DIASPORA

Blue-green watery globe
tugging to a red core
we are a distant comet,
white cloud of unburnished rocks,
frisking the heavens
for an arc
to earth, sea, home.

Green-brown Palestine,
cactus fruit and wild thyme,
olive orchards, cypress trees . . .
we travel on your mountain tops
tethered by voices from suitcases
and the yaw of blackened keys.

Blue-black night
silver stars of ancestors
traveling a displaced orbit
around a lost sun, repeating:
when will we see the colors of our land,
when will we land . . .

THE CEASEFIRE

She was a fish returning to the water!
She was a beautiful woman with a scratched face
Who bathed in the sun,
Unashamed of the wounds on her knees and the pain in
　　the heart!
She walks in the streets with the grace of a woman
And the speed of a warrior!
She inspects the windows and is stunned at the wreckage
She takes pictures of the ruins
And rejoices for the survivors
Dashing through the street
Saying the *Takbeer** for the destroyed minarets
She accounts her children
Stroking the heads of orphans and wiping their tears
She picks up her torn dress
And covers her burns!

---

* *Takbeer* translates to "God is greatest" and is used mainly by Muslims in prayer, calls to prayer during the Hajj, and expression of faith in times of joy or stress.

THE EARTH

The earth is not a ball
Not like a fist
Nor does it resemble a pear
Or a bean
Earth is a long way/road/path

❀

The earth,
is like our blind mother
and
We, are her broken compass.

WHO PLANTS THE HONEY?

Who plants the honey in your eyes,
And releases your birds from their cages?
Where can I escape with the remains of wild thyme
    which emanates your smell?
It was written on your cloud as the only route to joy
For my compass
And written on my heart
To bleed you whenever it is besieged
And to make you cry rain alone over the deserts of the
    world
Who will shower you with water poems?
How can you resemble waves?
Which end up as froth
It disappears without a trace
Then it is born again in memory forever!
Where does your face start?
Since you are the whole horizon?
Where does it end?
And it is the water,
It discharges me in its cups
And I take their form
Your face is like the burning edges,
The glow of tobacco when it burns in no other place but
    my chest

It is a combination of light,
A cosmic façade of special magic
The senses perceive it
It pays no attention to others but me
And your face,
My old song
In the crowd of discord,

My elaborate sculpture
In the falsehood of mirrors.
Gather the honey in your eyes
In big flashing jars,
And leave me the sand of the shore to build houses
Then gift them to the waves.

FROM THE HEART OF THE BATTLE

There,
We fight for a dream,
The dream of survival
Or
The dream of annihilation,
I don't know where I am
or how I am!
As if I am living the apocalypse
In the image of the dark nothingness

We fight for hope,
That hope,
The transparent one through which
our souls escape to white eternity,
The vague one through which
you unite with the terrifying loneliness,
And
The killed one on the margins of innocence
in the archive of fake history

We fight for humanity,
That doesn't recognise us
as human beings,
that refuses us,
our existence
our right of being
and
our faith in this land,

We fight for this forgotten people,
After they were betrayed by all

even by the alphabet,
After they were killed by all means
even by desperation,

And
After all that chaos,
I go back to ME,
Diving so deep
where the pain originates,
Where the wide universe
becomes too tight,
To kill me sometimes
and to revive me other times,

To say:
"From the heart of the battle,
I stand and fight,
Here I found myself
Here I knew myself
Here I was
Here I am
and certainly,
Here, I will be."

IT'S THE RESURRECTION

O world,
It's the resurrection,
In all forms and shapes,
With its violence,
arrogance and tyranny.
The exhausted men
stand under the blazing sun
for hours or for decades,
to fill a gallon of water
immersed with sweat and blood,
The gallon that is not enough
to even wash their dark nights,

While they're there,
they're losing their dignity,
after they lost their homes
and dreams,
They curse what remains
of their present
along with their memories,

They wander and scream,
Tears are pouring down
from them like sweat,
but
without the sound of weeping,

They break into this hell
without hesitation,
For the sake of their hungry children,
in those dilapidated tents,
Where the blazing sun

is savoring in torturing them
And earth in starving them,

After all that,
Despair continues
with them and inside them,
Without waking up to
a glimmer of hope
in the upcoming days . . .

In Gaza, the water queue is a form of "The
Postponed Death" in life.

DISPLACEMENT

It is the uprooting of memory
and the direct distortion
of the features of
the soul before the body,

It is to be torn apart
from the inside
before becoming
a pile of remains
on the outside,

It is to lose
your humanity and dignity
at every moment,
and as time passes,
you even lose yourself.

It is the unification with pain,
the coalescence with the inner scream,
the sick harmony with slow death,
and the crying without knowing the reason.
It is the sneaking killer
of every moment of joy
that you try to steal
from your miserable day.

Displacement is the eternal pain
that cannot be forgotten,
even if you forget yourself.

GAZA WILL RISE

From the ashes of despair, where shadows reign,
Gaza stirs beneath the weight of pain.
A land scorched by grief, yet still it dreams,
Through shattered streets, hope softly gleams.
The winds may howl, the skies may cry,
But Gaza's spirit will never die.
Through rubble and ruin, its pulse beats strong,
A melody of resilience, a timeless song.
Like a phoenix born from fire's embrace,
It will rise anew, reclaim its space.
Walls will crumble, but not the soul,
For Gaza's heart remains whole.
Children's laughter will pierce the air,
Seeds of peace will sprout with care.
The olive trees, with roots so deep,
Will tell of promises Gaza keeps.
Oh Gaza, your scars are stories of might,
Each wound is a testament to your fight.
Through darkest nights and longest years,
You rise above your deepest fears.
Let the world bear witness, let it be known,
That Gaza's fire cannot be overthrown.
From ashes to glory, it will ascend,
A beacon of hope that will never bend.
Gaza will rise, proud and free,
A testament to humanity's plea.
For from destruction, life will flow,
And Gaza's light will forever glow.

A NOTE ON THE EDITORS

NASEER H. ARURI (1934–2015) was a scholar-activist and expert on Middle East politics, US foreign policy in the Middle East, and human rights. Born in Jerusalem, Aruri came to the US in 1954. Aruri was Chancellor Professor of Political Science at the University of Massachusetts Dartmouth. He was a member on the Palestinian National Council (PNC), the parliament-in-exile of the Palestinian people and decision-making body of the Palestine Liberation Organization (PLO), and sat on the PLO's Central Council. He was a founding member of the Arab Organization for Human Rights and served on the board of directors of Amnesty International USA, Human Rights Watch/Middle East, the International Institute for Criminal Investigations at The Hague, and *Third World Quarterly*. He was the author and editor of numerous books, including *Occupation: Israel Over Palestine* (AAUG Press, ZED Press); *The Obstruction of Peace: The US, Israel and the Palestinians* (Common Courage Press); *Palestinian Refugees: The Right of Return* (Pluto); *Revising Culture, Reinventing Peace: The Influence of Edward W. Said* (Interlink Books); and *Dishonest Broker: The US Role in Israel/Palestine* (South End Press, 2003). His papers have been preserved at the University of Massachusetts Dartmouth's Claire T. Carney Library Archives and Special Collections.

EDMUND GHAREEB is a scholar, journalist, and internationally recognized expert on the Middle East, Arab and American media, US-Arab relations, and international affairs. He has taught at Georgetown University, George Washington University, the

University of Virginia, Pepperdine University, and McGill University. He launched the first regularly offered courses on Kurdish history, politics, and society in the US. He was the American University Center for Global Peace's first Mustafa Barzani Distinguished Scholar in Kurdish Studies and served as coordinator for the Middle East program at AU's School of International Service. He is former president of the Association of Arab-American University Graduates, former vice president of the Shaybani Society of International Law and the American Foreign Policy Institute, and an advisory board member of the Institute of Middle Eastern and North African affairs.

Dr. Ghareeb is the author of several widely acclaimed books, including *War in the Gulf, 1990–91* (Oxford University Press), *The Kurdish Question in Iraq* (Syracuse University Press), *Split Vision: The Portrayal of Arabs in the American Media* (Middle East Policy Council), and coauthor of *Historical Dictionary of Iraq* (Scarecrow Press). He is the former assistant editor of the *Journal of Palestine Studies* and was an advisory board member of the *Middle East Journal*. He has lectured widely—in the US, Europe, the Arab world, Brazil, and China—and served as reviewer for the UN Development Programme. He was a Washington correspondent for *The Beirut Daily Star, Al-Hayat, Al-Ittihad,* and *Emirates News* and a contributor to *Al-Mustaqbal* (Paris). He has been a contributing analyst to the Associated Press, Fr24, the BBC, *Al-Jazeera,* and Abu Dhabi TV and is a frequent commentator and analyst for numerous media outlets. He has also been interviewed by numerous US media outlets including PBS NewsHour, NPR, C-Span, ABC, CNN, and other American outlets.

The translations of the majority of poems in this volume are the work of Naseer Aruri and Edmund Ghareeb.

ACKNOWLEDGMENTS

This anthology is the result of a shared labor of love, memory, and resistance. It would not have seen the light of day without the unwavering support, wisdom, and generosity of so many—far too many to name individually, but each deeply appreciated.

I would like to begin by expressing my appreciation and thanks to Seven Stories Press, especially founder Dan Simon, editorial assistant Sofia DeSanto, and former managing editor Tal Milovina Mancini, for their enthusiasm, creative insight, patience, and unwavering support for this new edition.

A special word of appreciation goes to Daphne Muse, Charlie Cobb, Jennifer Lawson, Courtland Cox, Ann Holloway, Judy Richardson, and Curtis Hayes (later Muhammad) for their roles with Drum & Spear Press, which published the first edition of *Enemy of the Sun*. Daphne Muse in particular was instrumental in calling for this republication and has been a tireless advocate for the book and its message. This press, which first took a chance on the work when others declined, played a crucial role in its history.

Additionally, I am indebted to Dr. Greg Thomas for his illuminating introduction in this edition and for shedding light on the profound connection between Sameeh Al-Qassem and the late African American author and revolutionary George Jackson. Jackson wrote two books in prison, *Soledad Brother* and *Blood in My Eye*. He was later killed by prison guards. Thomas' scholarship on Jackson's prison library helped rekindle interest in this work. Sameeh Al-Qassem's poem "Enemy of the Sun" was found and mistakenly published under Jackson's name following his death. I had separately translated and published the poem in

The Torch, an intercollegiate student magazine; the *Sophian*, the Smith College student newspaper; *Dialog*, the graduate student journal at Georgetown University; and *The Georgetown Voice*, a student newspaper. This unintended mistake shows the legacy of solidarity between Palestinian and Black liberation movements. It especially reveals the powerful resonance felt by readers. This is a testament to that shared spirit in the struggle for justice, human rights, and resistance to oppression.

I also owe special thanks to professor, editor, and journalist Carl Senna, whose long-standing support helped bring this work to life and who helped promote the book when he did the first radio interview in New York with me and Lebanese journalist Raghida Dergham. He also collaborated with Naseer in the translation and publication of several poems in *The Boston Phoenix* and *Ploughshares*. Appreciation and thanks are extended to the publishers of these magazines for granting permission to reprint those poems.

Special thanks go to Ms. Ruqyah Sweidan for her diligent research and writing of the poets' and translators' biographies which enrich the new edition of the book. I appreciate the contributions of the poets whose works were newly added to this edition—Zeina Azzam, Samar Najia, Hend Joudat, Dr. Ali Ibrahim Al-Tawil, Ahmed Mansour, Manar Harb, Abdul Wahab Al-Bayyaty, Kamal Nasser, Wadi'a Nasser, Iliya Abu Chedid, Kamel Abu Jaber, Salem Jubran, Laila Al Jammal—whose voices have added depth and resonance.

I'd like to extend a special acknowledgment to Gabriel Johnson, a recent graduate of the University of Massachusetts Dartmouth, whose enthusiasm for the book led him to bring it into classroom discussions, organize poetry readings, and create pamphlets introducing the poems to new readers.

I am deeply grateful to the translators whose voices brought these poems into English and made them accessible to new audiences: In the first edition, Hatem Hussaini for "From Behind the Bars" by Fadwa Touqan; "Truth is Said" by Yusif Hamdan;

"I Defy" and "The Children of Rafah" by Sameeh Al-Qassem; "From Diaries of a Fighter" by Abdel Rahman Muhammad Rafie; and "Jail and Children," "Tent #50," and "Song of a Refugee" by Rashed Hussein (with Ann Lavee, wife of Hussein); and Ali Arouri for "A Poem to Mahmoud Darweesh" by Arshad Tawfiq. In the second edition, Edmund Ghareeb for "The Arab" by Kamel Abu Jaber, "Shelter No. 20" and "Barbed Wire" by Abdul Wahab Al-Bayyaty, "To My Mother" by Kamal Nasser, "My Son Kamal" by Wadi'a Nasser, "The House" by Iliya Abu Chedid, "The Massacred Village" by Salem Jubran, and "They Taught Me" by Laila Al Jammal; and Ruqyah Sweidan for "The Ceasefire" and "The Earth" by Hend Joudat.

In recognition of those who contributed to the first edition, I remember and honor those no longer with us, whose support was vital: Dr. Ibrahim Abu-Lughod and Dr. Hatem Husseini—professors, activists, and friends whose support and suggestions were invaluable.

The first edition is indebted to Professor Samuel Allen of Wesleyan University for writing a most valuable preface and Dr. Vernon Ingrahm at Southeastern Massachusetts University for helpful suggestions and comments. I am grateful to Ms. Lucinda Shastid, whose early help and support during the translation and publication process of the first edition made a lasting impact. I acknowledge the contributions of Nabila Mango, formerly of Harvard's Widener Library Middle East Division; Naim Issa and Antoun Moussa of the Library of Congress Middle East Section; and Huda Karaman, who was one of the people to introduce us to Drum & Spear Press. I am grateful for the contributions of Helen Mead and Rita Girard of Southeastern Massachusetts University for typing part of the original manuscript. Appreciation is also due to Palestinian organizations and presses which have permitted us to use material from their publications.

And last but not least, I owe an unpayable debt to Professor Naseer Aruri, my late friend, co-editor, co-translator, and fellow traveler on this journey. It was Naseer who first encouraged me to pursue this book project after reading my translations. We shared a belief in the power of poetry to bridge the world and that people of different cultures, ethnicities, and religions could be brought closer to each other through this work. His vision lives on in these pages. I am also grateful to his wife Mrs. Joyce Aruri, his son Jamal Aruri, Esq., and his daughter Professor Karen Aruri Carnes for their steadfast support and their commitment to seeing this new edition come to life.

ABOUT THE POETS

Known as the national poet of Palestine, MAHMOUD DAR-WEESH (1941–2008) was a highly revered literary figure with many admirers across the Arab world. Thousands of people would regularly attempt to attend his readings only to be "turned away for lack of space."

Darweesh experienced devastating events in his early life. At the tender age of seven, he and his family were expelled from their village of al-Birweh during the Nakba and were forced to take refuge in Lebanon. A year later, the Darweesh family re-entered Occupied Palestine as "present-absent aliens," after the state of Israel completed the census of the remaining Palestinian Arabs. Since Darweesh lacked documentation of his newly imposed identity, he was particularly vulnerable to Israeli repression. He endured several terms of imprisonment and house arrest for his poetry as well as for traveling within the country without a permit, a rule strictly imposed on Arab citizens during Israeli military rule (1948–1966) prior to the occupation of the remainder Palestinian—as well as Syrian—Territories (1967). In *Journal of an Ordinary Grief* (Yawmiyyat al-Huzn al-Aadi), Darweesh bitterly concludes: "you realize that philosophically you exist but legally you do not."

One of Darweesh's most profound prose poems, "Memory for Forgetfulness," is so named for two concepts: "memory" refers to his constantly tethered movement due to Israel's restrictions and his rhythmic return to his life in the homeland, while "forgetfulness" signifies the impact of Israel's 1982 Invasion of Lebanon and siege of Beirut.

RASHED HUSSEIN (1936–1977) was a Palestinian American poet. Born in Musmus (Haifa district), Palestine, Hussein attended primary school in the neighboring town of Umm al-Fahm before completing his secondary education in Nazareth. There he became a teacher, educating students from poor, rural backgrounds. Hussein began writing poetry in 1952, and published his first poetry collection in 1954. By 1959, he had translated several Arabic poems into Hebrew and vice versa, as well as the works of well-known international poets such as Bertolt Brecht of Germany, Nazim Hikmet of Turkey, and the Congolese leader Patrice Lumumba. Hussein also edited the weekly newspapers *Al-Musawwar* and *Al-Fajr*. The latter was associated with the Histadrut Workers Union, an Israeli labor organization founded in 1920.

In 1962, Hussein met Ann Lavee, a Jewish American woman who was married to an officer in the Israeli army. They soon fell in love, and Hussein took her to meet his family in Musmus. Lavee traveled to the US in 1965, where she studied at Ohio State University, and Hussein followed in January of 1966. Hussein was horrified at the events of the Naksa in 1967. The couple spent that year traveling in Montreal, Niagara Falls, and Washington, DC, before marrying in October 1967. They moved to New York in 1969, where Hussein enrolled at NYU and volunteered as a translator, lecturer, and poetry reader at the Palestinian Liberation Organization and the Arab League.

The writings of Rashed Hussein illustrate the tragic effects of war on his people and were acclaimed by writers in both the Arab and Jewish communities. At the same time, he often criticized the policies of Ben-Gurion, the first prime minister of Israel, as well as those of later Israeli governments. His published collections of poetry include *Ma' al-fajr* (At Dawn) (1957) and *Ana al-ard la tahrimini al-matar* (I'm the Earth, Don't Deny Me the Rain) (1976).

Hussein died from smoke inhalation from a fire started by a cigarette. His body was discovered in his New York City apartment and flown back to Palestine. At Ben Gurion Airport, his family waited to receive their loved one, watching patiently through the airport window since they were barred from entering the arrival area. An ambulance transferred Hussein to Musmus, where family, friends, visitors, and admirers of his work attended his funeral. Thousands of people flooded the town. Hussein's ailing father made a humble speech, thanking the crowd for attending. Sameeh Al-Qassem was among the men who carried Hussein's body to its final resting place on a hilltop cemetery. In New York, a memorial service was arranged by the PLO at the UN Church Center, and was also attended by many of his friends.

SAMEEH AL-QASSEM (1939–2014) was one of Palestine's most cherished poets, hailing from the village of Al Rameh in Galilee. He was born in Zarqa, in then-Transjordan. It is said that as an infant, while on a journey from Zarqa to Palestine, Al-Qassem began to cry in his father's arms. The rest of the group feared that the baby's wails would reveal their location to the Axis powers' warplanes that circled overhead, so much so that they threatened to kill the child, until his father pointed his weapon at them. As a grown man, Al-Qassem used to recount this story, saying: "People have been trying to shut me up ever since I was a baby, but I'll show them! I will speak at the top of my voice, whenever and for however long I want—and no one will silence me!"

Al-Qassem attended primary school in Al Rameh and secondary school in Nazareth, where he met many poets and writers raised in the aftermath of the Nakba, including Rashed Hussein, Shakib Jahshan, and Taha Muhammad Ali. Al-Qassem wrote his early poetry in schoolbooks and letters to his friends. After he completed his education, Al-Qassem was required to enlist in the Israeli Army, as his family belonged to the Druze community, who were subject to conscription. In protest, Al-Qassem founded the "Free Druze Youth," a political organization for young Druze men who refused the draft. The members organized many protests and enjoyed widespread popular support. Al-Qassem was arrested by Israeli authorities, who later released him for fear that his defiance would encourage other young men to follow his example. Al-Qassem never joined the military.

Al-Qassem was one of several Palestinian poets and orators who expressed their rejection of Israeli policy by reciting resistance-themed poetry at public village gatherings. He became a published poet at the age of eighteen, and many of his early poems articulate the cruel treatment endured by Palestinians at the hands of the Israelis. Later, his writings took on a more philosophical and idealistic tone, such as in his long poems called *sarbiyyat*. In this style of poetry, a more free-flowing speech is blended with references to culture. His lyrical poetry describes the richness of Palestinian culture and heritage. Despite periods of constant hardship and violence against the Palestinians, Al-Qassem's poetry remained, to his people, "like a lifeboat to a drowning man, and the poet's voice rang out laden with sadness and ire, and full of pagan fire."

TAWFIQ ZAYYAD (1929–1994) was both a poet and prominent political figure. He was born in Nazareth, one of the major cities of northern Palestine, where he would later become mayor. Zayyad was married to Na'ila Yusuf Sabbagh and had four children: Wahiba, Amin, Ubur, and Faris. Growing up, Zayyad studied in Nazareth government schools while helping his father, Mr. Amin Zayyad, in his grocery store. His interest in politics began at school, as his teachers regularly distributed issues of *Al-Ittihad* and *al-Mihmaz* to their pupils. His poetry, first published in the late 1940s, became the medium through which he expressed the struggles he experienced in his career and within the Palestinian liberation movement, his views on class and the world, and other issues important to his people. Known for having immense depth yet being simple to memorize, several of his poems were set to music and became part of the popular musical heritage of the resistance.

Zayyad was an active organizer in student demonstrations against the impending Zionist conquest as well as a member of the Nazareth branch of the National Liberation League in Palestine. Following the Nakba, he joined the Israeli Communist Party (later known as Rakah), founded in October of 1948. Zayyad's activism continued for several years, with him participating in trade union actions in Nazareth, working with the Arab Workers Congress, and writing articles on behalf of Histadrut in Haifa's *Al-Ittihad* newspaper about the experiences and conditions of Arab laborers.

Zayyad also integrated his poetry into moving political speeches, which often instigated repression from the Israeli authorities. He was imprisoned in 1954 following a speech he gave called *Araba*, in which he protested the policies of the Israeli government. Upon his release, he was regarded popularly as a champion for his people's rights and his poetry came to be prolific. He would be arrested several more times in the following years for his continued actions. In response to increased Israeli confiscation of Palestinian land in Galilee in 1976, Zayyad, along with fellow members of the Rakah, called for a national strike, which would later become an honored anniversary still observed by Palestinians (through strikes and land protection action) today: *Land Day.*

SALEM JUBRAN (1941–2011) was born in Al Bukay'a, a village in Galilee. The Palestinian poet living in Israel was active in politics, journalism, and education. His articles appeared in several Israeli outlets such as *Haaretz, Yedioth Ahronoth*, and *Maariv* as well as the Lebanese *Al Nahar*. He was also editor of *Al-Ittihad*, considered Israel's most important Arabic-language daily, and *Al-Jadid*, a popular magazine on literature and culture. Jubran was senior lecturer at the Center for Humanistic Education at the Lohamei Hagetaot Holocaust Museum, located in Western Galilee. He was also involved with the Jewish-Arab peace center in Givat Haviva, north of Tel Aviv, and was a member of the Israeli Communist Party.

Through his poetry, Jubran urged his fellow poets to tirelessly commit themselves to Palestinian liberation. In his piece, "The Singer of the Revolution," he writes: "It is my fate to sing. To hunger. And remain singing. For my wounds to bleed. And remain singing. If I die in battle. The songs, Among the comrades, will take my place. And fight for me." In another poem,

"Announcer for the Wind and Rain," he cites the eternity of the written word as recompense for loss of property: "In my village, / You can plough all the houses of my village / Without a trace, / You can take my rebec / And burn it, having cut its string, / You can . . . / But you cannot strangle my tune / For I am the lover of the land / Singer for the wind and rain." Jubran was laid to rest in his hometown in December 2011.

NIZAR QABBANI (1923–1998) was one of the most famous Arab poets of the twentieth century. He was born in Damascus, and his father was a nationalist activist involved in Syria's struggle for independence. His paternal grandfather was a famous poet, composer, and actor credited for influencing modern Egyptian theatre. Growing up in such an intellectual household gave Qabbani the potential for great artistic and political expression. He graduated from the University of Damascus with a degree in law and went on to become a member of the foreign service, working as a diplomat in the Syrian embassies in Egypt, Turkey, Lebanon, Britain, China, and Spain.

Qabbani published his first collection, *The Brunette Said To Me* (Qalat li al-Samra), in 1942 at the age of nineteen. In those verses, he passionately describes the beauty and desirability of a woman. He continued to write similar verses in his first four collections. There were several more pieces included in *Qaṣāʾid min Nizār Qabbānī* (Poems by Nizar Qabbani), and others, in which he expressed his resentment of patriarchal norms and advocated social reforms for women. Included in this collection is one of his best-known national poems, "Bread, Hashish and Moon" (Khubz, hashish wa gamar), in which he exposes the corruption and adverse traits that hold back Arab society. Qabbani had clearly emerged as a literary figure who dared to challenge social norms. Following the devastating Arab defeat in the Six-Day War, however, Qabbani shifted away from his love-themed poems and began to write more nationalist poetry that was laced with anger toward the Arab leaders. One of his long poems, "Marginal Notes in the Book of the Setback" (Hawdmish'ala daftar al-Naksa), admonished those leaders he felt were responsible for the loss. Qabbani's poetic style has been described as "written from the heart, in a simple, economical style," emphasizing the rhythms of the Syrian dialect. Qabbani was known as a "politician in poetry."

FADWA TOUQAN (1917–2003) was a Palestinian poet from Nablus. Born to a distinguished family, her brother Ibrahim, a well-known Palestinian nationalist poet, was her main teacher in poetry. Touqan's early adulthood coincided with remarkable social change and political devastation. Following the 1948 Nakba, thousands of Palestinians fled east, bringing with them the norms and practices of their homeland. Nablus became a place that combined the tendencies of Jaffa, Haifa, West Jerusalem, and other culturally rich cities. In some ways, social change was spurred, and young, educated women began interacting more regularly with men. "When the roof fell on Palestine, the veil fell off the face of the Nablus woman," Touqan wrote. It was also during this tumultuous year that her father passed away. But with the departure of her stricter parent, Touqan also felt a greater sense of freedom.

Touqan lived in England from 1962 to 1964, studying English language and literature at Oxford University, then traveled throughout Europe and the Middle East. One of the themes Touqan explores in her writing is the the struggle of women in a patriarchal society, famously linking that struggle to Palestine's quest for liberation. In her poem "Hamzah," she writes, "This land is a woman," comparing the precious land of the Palestinians to a woman's resilience. Following the Six-Day War and Israel's occupation of the remaining lands of historic Palestine, Touqan's poetry became more politically oriented and nationalist. The Israeli general Moshe Dayan once compared the prowess of her poetry to the strength of twenty Israeli commandos. After her poetry was translated into English in the 1980s, her work became accessible to a wider audience and Arab Americans came to read her work to reconnect with their heritage.

Touqan was the recipient of numerous accolades, among them poetry prizes from Italy, Greece, and Jordan as well as the Jerusalem Award for Culture and the Arts and the Honorary Palestine Prize for Poetry. In 2003, during the Second Intifada, Touqan passed away in her hometown of Nablus under Israeli siege.

ARSHAD TAWFIQ was born in 1944 and graduated from the college of law at Baghdad University. He served as an ambassador of Iraq from 1979 to 1991 and was stationed in Cuba, Haiti, Spain, Mexico, and The Vatican. He also served as editor of several Iraqi magazines and was the head of Iraq's National Radio Service. He published his first poetry collection, *Al Najm wa Al Darweesh* (The Star and The Devoted/Ascetic), in 1967. His second collection, *Al Wuqoof Kharej Al Asma'a* (Standing Outside of Names), followed in 1973.

YUSIF HAMDAN was born in 1942 in Jaljulia, in northern Palestine. His surname belongs to the larger Shreim family hailing from Qalqilya, who owned a home in the village of Jaljulia. In 1948, the Hamdan family lost contact with their relatives in Qalqilya following the area's occupation by Israeli forces. Hamdan completed primary school in Jaljulia and secondary school in Tira, another city in northern Palestine.

Hamdan was a teacher at a primary school in Daliyat al-Karmel, Haifa, where the poet Sameeh Al-Qassem also taught. The two became close friends and remained so throughout their time in Haifa. At the time, Mahmoud Darweesh was editor of *Al-Jadeed,* the magazine of the Communist Party. Hamdan joined Darweesh and Al-Qassem in publishing his poetry in *Al-Jadeed* and *Al-Ittihad,* which angered the ruling class. Shortly after, Hamdan and Al-Qassem were dismissed from their teaching positions. They celebrated at Darweesh's home.

Hamdan returned to The Triangle, a cluster of Palestinian towns (including Jaljulia and Tira) adjacent to the present-day Green Line bordering the West Bank. Later, he traveled to New

York where he worked in the office of the Palestine Liberation Organization (PLO), then as a researcher in the Research Center of the PLO in Beirut. After the outbreak of the Lebanese Civil War, Hamdan returned to New York, advising on the Libyan and the Qatari missions. He worked in the Information Department of the United Nations Secretariat until his retirement.

ABDEL RAHMAN MUHAMMAD RAFIE (1936–2015) was a Bahraini poet. During his lifetime, he published nine collections of deeply expressive yet colloquial poetry. This mixed style contributed to his popularity in the Gulf region. His best-known collections include *Songs of the Four Seas*, *Circling around the Distant*, and *She Has the Laughter of Roses*.

In an anthology compiled by Rafie, he asserted that poetry in the colloquial dialect was best enjoyed heard rather than read. He recommended that readers immerse themselves in the Bahraini culture and dialect to understand the message behind his poems.

Rafie's poem "Palestine Speaks" describes the extreme pain he felt over the tragedy of the Palestinian people. He also stressed the severity of their physical and emotional suffering, emphasizing themes of sacrifice and steadfastness. "The great wound is roaring, and let it burn like red hell, and let the atmosphere over me shed its fire, and let my space be filled with woe, and let the world witness the movement of a nation that has risen despite disease and enemies," he wrote.

HADIA ABDUL-HADI was passionate about literature since she was a child. She considered reading to be nourishment for her mind, heart, and soul. While working as a host for the Near East Arab Radio Station, she regularly expressed her thoughts and observations, forming her perspectives from carefully conducted research and then bringing them to the ear of the world. She was interested in social issues, and analyzed the role of women in society, refusing a "partisan method between the sexes" and instead attributing gender oppression to both men and women.

She made it her mission to enhance and broaden storytelling in literature to her audience—in her words, "to direct my efforts to a living aspect of literature that is still neglected in our dear Palestine, namely 'the story.'"

FAWZI JIRYIS ABDULLAH (1942–1988) was born in Nazareth. He graduated with distinction from the University of Haifa, earning a degree in Arabic, followed by a master's degree from Tel Aviv University. He was a teacher at a school in Nazareth.

Abdullah authored five major collections of poetry, totaling more than seventy poems. He used to include the name of the month during which each collection was drafted to indicate each period of the harrowing massacre of Palestinians by Israelis. April referenced the Deir Yassin Massacre. May marked the end of the British Mandate and the establishment of the State of Israel. December was the start of the First Intifada. Abdullah founded a cultural organization as well as *Al-Mawakeb* magazine. He expressed his love of freedom, his homeland, and his people with great passion. He also deeply treasured the Arabic language. He was known for his generous personality and tireless fervor.

KAMEL ABU JABER (1932–2020) was a Jordanian scholar, politician, and diplomat. In the Jordanian government, Jaber served as minister of economics in 1973 and minister of foreign affairs from 1991 to 1993. He was president of the Jordan Institute of Diplomacy (1997–2001), professor of political science at the University of Jordan (1971–1985), associate professor of political science at Smith College (1967–1969), and visiting professor at the Carter Center of Emory University (1989). Dr. Jaber has written numerous books on Jordan, Israel, Syria, and Palestine, and led the Jordanian-Palestinian delegation to the 1991 Madrid Conference, the first internationally sponsored event for Arab-Israeli peace negotiations.

ABDUL WAHAB AL-BAYYATY (1926–1999) was one of the twentieth century's leading Arab poets and one of Iraq's most important revolutionary poets; his works, which centered on themes of exile, alienation, and social and political change, were widely acclaimed. Born in Baghdad, he earned a degree in Arabic language and literature from the University of Baghdad's Teachers Training College in 1950. He taught briefly in Iraq and published several poetry collections including *Mala'ika wa shayatin* (Angels and Devils, 1950); *Abariq muhashshama* (Broken Pitchers, 1954); *Ash'ar fi al-manfa* (Poetry in Exile, 1957); and *Love, Death & Exile: Poems Translated from Arabic* (1991), among others. His leftist views and disagreements with the Iraqi monarchy and, later, the Republican government led to his extended exile from Iraq. He passed away in Damascus, Syria, but always longed to return to his homeland.

KAMAL NASSER (1924–1973) was a highly revered Palestinian political activist and writer whose works emphasized Arab Unity and Palestinian resistance against the Israeli Occupation. He was born in Gaza, raised in Birzeit, and obtained degrees in political science and law. He later worked as a college professor and launched the first Palestinian Ba'ath Party paper and established the weekly magazine, *Al-Jil Al-Jadid* (The New Generation). Expelled from the West Bank by Israel in the Occupation of 1967, Nasser joined the Palestinian Liberation Organization (PLO) in 1968 and served in several executive positions. He became editor of the PLO periodical *Falastin Al Thawra* (Palestine of the Revolution). Among his works were *Jirah Tughanni* (Singing Wounds, 1959) and *Ughniyat Min Paris* (Songs from Paris, 1967). Nasser, along with two other prominent PLO members, Kamal Adwan and Muhammad Yousef An-Najjar, was assassinated in 1973 by a team of undercover Israeli commandos in a night raid on his home in Beirut, Lebanon.

WADI'A NASSER was born in Birzeit in 1891 and graduated from the Friends School in 1909. She was a cultured woman who spoke English and wrote both poetry and prose. She was a loving mother who devotedly raised her children, the youngest of whom was Kamal Nasser. Wadi'a Nasser believed in Kamal's exceptional literary talent and encouraged him in his pursuits until the news of his assassination in 1973 in Beirut. She expressed her grief, devastation, and pride in her son in her poem, "My Son Kamal," which was published on the front page of *Al Fajr* newspaper after he died. She spoke often of Kamal and her memories of him until she passed away nearly five years later.

The poet ILIYA ABU CHEDID (1934–1998) was born in the town of Mtayleb, north of Beirut. Iliya lost his parents at a very young age and went into the care of his uncle, Boutros Abu Chedid. Iliya studied at the National Youth School in Al-Fraikah, then at the Apostles Institute in Jounieh until the age of sixteen. He immigrated to Ghana in 1950 and worked in trade. He was in and out of his country over the years due to instability but finally resettled in Lebanon in 1981. Lebanese colloquial poetry magazines featured Abu Chedid's early poetry on their front pages, and he won first place in two prominent poetry competitions.

LAILA AL JAMMAL (1942–2024) was born in Akka, northern Palestine. She was a prominent poet, humanitarian, and activist. She presented and produced programs on Arab and Palestinian culture and heritage and worked as an information advisor at the Arab League office in Washington. During the 1982 Israeli invasion of Lebanon, Al Jammal volunteered with the Palestinian Red Crescent, coordinating medical support and international relations between the Palestinian Red Crescent and the International Red Cross and giving the profits from her poetry books to the Palestinian Red Crescent. Al Jammal organized the first Palestinian cultural and art exhibit at the United Nations as well as in several American cities. She then became Palestinian Authority Television and Radio's director of international relations and later worked as director of the department of international relations in President Arafat's office. She published a number of books and articles on Palestinian politics, media, and heritage.

SAMAR NAJIA is an Arab American poet. Born in Lebanon, she is a graduate of Georgetown University and presently resides in Virginia. Samar writes about the intergenerational trauma inherent to the Palestinian diaspora; the hidden and lingering scars from wars, flight, and exile. She seeks to use her poetry to humanize and give a voice to the often silenced and devalued victims of the genocide in Gaza. She has written two manuscripts—a mixed poetry and prose memoir about the trauma inherent to the repeated displacement of her Jerusalem-born mother and a personal narrative about domestic abuse in an immigrant household.

WALID KEILANI was born in Nablus, Palestine in 1938. He received a master of science degree in economics from Utah State University in 1968 and a bachelor's degree from Ain Shams University in Egypt in 1961. He is an economist and businessperson who has worked at the World Bank in Washington DC, the Arab Fund for Economic and Social Development, and Alshall Economic Consultants in Kuwait. Keilani has written poetry books and songs in both Arabic and English and has received several awards for his writing. He is a well-known poet whose many poems were turned into songs. His poems thematically center freedom, human rights, justice, and peace; and his two children's poetry books comprise whimsical takes on nature and history.

MANAR HARB is a researcher, poet, and artist born in 1985 in Ramallah, Palestine. She attended the Friends School in Ramallah and obtained her BA in business administration and marketing from the University of South Florida (2008) as well as an MFA in book art and creative writing at Mills College in Oakland, California. Her artwork combines nature, language, and bodily forms, yielding abstract aerial forms that have spiritual embodiments. Language is at the forefront of her research, whereby she explores meanings and messages derived from characters in the Arabic alphabet and illustrates them through literal, visual, and performative means. She has published articles, features, and poems in both English and Arabic.

HAROUN HASHEM RASHID (1927–2020) was a Palestinian poet born in Al-Zaytoun neighborhood in Gaza City. While he composed his poetry through the 1950s, Rashid became known as one of the poets of the Nakba; his words were laced with a strong spirit of rebellion and revolution. Rashid published at least twenty poetry collections in his life and also wrote poetic plays. He worked as an educator, as the alternate representative of Palestine in the Arab League, and as overseer of the Palestine Liberation Organization's media office in Gaza between 1965 and 1967. He received several honorable accolades, among them the Jerusalem Medal for Culture, Arts, and Letters from the Palestinian President in 2016 and the Sharjah Arab Poetry Festival Award in 2014.

ZEINA AZZAM, a Palestinian American poet, writer, editor, and community activist, is the poet laureate of the City of Alexandria, Virginia (2022–2025). She holds an MA in Arabic literature from Georgetown University. Since 2016, she has served as a mentor for We Are Not Numbers, a writing program for youth in Gaza, and is currently the poetry editor for the organization. Her publications include the full-length poetry collection *Some Things Never Leave You* (2023) and the chapbook *Bayna Bayna, In-Between* (2021), in addition to poems in literary journals and anthologies.

HEND JOUDAT was born in Al Bureij Refugee Camp in Gaza on August 15, 1983. Her first anthology, *Someone Always Leaves*, was published in 2013 by Mosaic Press in Amman. Her more recent work, *No Sugar in the City*, was published by Al-Ahlia Publishing and Distribution in Amman. She has also written numerous poems and short stories as well as scripts for several documentaries. Joudat hosted a program, *Sabah el Khair ya Watan* (Good Morning, Homeland). She won the gold prize at the Arab Youth Cultural Festival in Cairo in 2006.

DR. ALI IBRAHIM AL-TAWIL was born and raised in Gaza City. He is a refugee whose origins go back to the village of Al-Maghar, Ramla City, from which his grandparents were displaced during the Nakba in 1948. A prominent doctor, Al-Tawil has been practicing at Al-Aqsa Martyrs Hospital since 2022. Having witnessed the Second Intifada in 2000, the internal Palestinian division and the civil war in 2007, followed by the fierce wars against the Gaza Strip in 2008, 2012, 2014, and 2021, and the recent war of 2023, Al-Tawil developed a political awareness that he translated through his pen, writing many poems describing the suffering of his people to the world.

AHMED MANSOUR was born and raised in a refugee camp in Gaza. Currently based in the US, he is a graduate of the NYU Arthur L. Carter Journalism Institute's News and Documentary Program and runs his own production company specializing in short videos. He worked as a translator and guide for international journalists covering the 2014 Gaza War and produced a series of short films highlighting the humanitarian crisis in the Gaza Strip that resulted from successive Israeli attacks. Ahmed was also a reporter for the Washington Report on the Middle East Affairs in Washington, DC, and has received residencies and fellowships from Duke University and the Paths to Peace Leadership Program.

PERMISSIONS